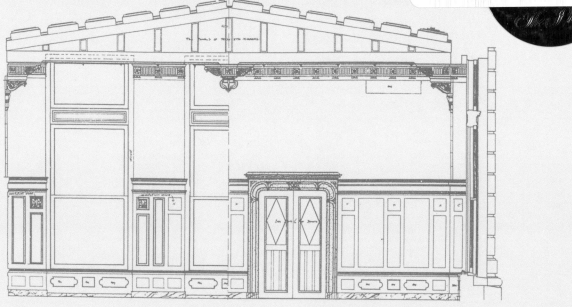

EAST ELEVATION   WEST ELEVATION

· ONE HALF INCH SCALE EAST AND WEST ELEVATIONS OF CAFÉ ·

· THE PLAZA ·

· H J Hardenbergh, Arch't ·   Nº 1 West 34th St NYC

288·6

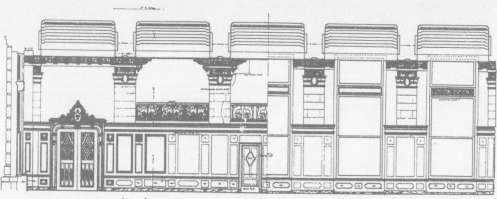

SOUTH ELEVATION   NORTH ELEVATION

· ONE HALF INCH SCALE NORTH AND SOUTH ELEVATIONS OF CAFÉ ·

· THE PLAZA ·

· H J Hardenbergh, Arch't ·   Nº 1 West 34th St NYC ·

At The Plaza

At The Plaza

~ An Illustrated History ~
of the World's Most Famous Hotel

Curtis Gathje

St. Martin's Press ❈ New York

www.stmartins.com

DESIGN BY JAMES SINCLAIR

ISBN 0-312-26174-8

First Edition: October 2000

10   9   8   7   6   5   4   3   2   1

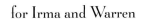

for Irma and Warren

Contents

The Plaza, the Camera, and the Century

*T*his photographic tribute to The Plaza was assembled at the close of the twentieth century. While it is most certainly a history of this renowned hotel, it is also a book about that century—albeit seen from a rather precise vantage point: 53,726 square feet of land situated on an island off North America. This plot of land is like no other in the world; indeed, it's hard to imagine many other places that have witnessed the last hundred years quite the way it has.

Early on, the land had an unremarkable history. Farmland originally, most of it was covered by a large pond used as an ice-skating rink in the winter. In 1890, an eight-story hotel, The Plaza, was erected there, which, with typical New York impatience, was declared outmoded after a mere fifteen years and demolished. In its place rose today's Plaza, whose doors opened October 1, 1907. Designed as a lavish pleasure palace, it has managed to maintain an aura of luxury and civility throughout the tumult of the century.

From the start, it has been a mirror of the New York scene. The city's changing tastes in design, restaurants, parties, and accommodations are reflected here, as well as its adjustments to servant shortages, Prohibition, the Great Depression, two world wars, the Cold War, women's rights, smokers' rights, animal rights, and even British rock and roll. The first guests to sign the register, Mr. and Mrs. Alfred Gwynne Vanderbilt, set the standard for the kind of people who would frequent it, luminaries who would reflect the changing definition of celebrity over the century—from Mark Twain and Diamond Jim Brady to F. Scott Fitzgerald, Marlene Dietrich, Frank Lloyd Wright, and the Beatles. (Ironically, one of the hotel's best-known residents, a mischievous six-year-old named Eloise, is entirely fictitious.) Over the years, the hotel's renown has grown to such an extent that The Plaza has become a symbol of elegance and refinement in American culture, inspiring writers from Neil Simon to Don DeLillo, artists from Everett Shinn to Red Grooms, and filmmakers from Alfred Hitchcock to Mike Nichols. Formal recognition of its cultural status came when it was designated a New York City landmark in 1969 and a National Historic Landmark in 1986.

The photographic process was introduced in 1839. Technology advanced slowly in those days, and it wasn't until the turn of the century that photography began to evolve more rapidly. In a way, then, the camera and The Plaza grew up together. Almost all of the photographs presented in this book were taken on-site, and aside from their documentary information, they also reflect what was considered suitable photographic material over the last hundred years. The earliest surviving pictures of the hotel rarely depict people: Apparently, it was not considered proper to be photographed in hotels, and, more significantly, the explosive flash powder used for lighting didn't inspire many willing subjects. By the century's end, however, most of the extant pictures depict *only* people, now quite eager to be portrayed against the backdrop of The Plaza. They would be pictured here for a variety of reasons as several new kinds of photographs—the publicity still, the paparazzi photograph, the photo op—made themselves known.

This picture collection also dispels the long-held myth that The Plaza has always been a sacrosanct temple of Beaux-Arts architecture. Although its exterior has changed little since 1907, the interior has undergone many alterations in order to remain fashionable and contemporary. Thus some very different (and unexpected) design trends can be seen here: German Renaissance architecture (in the Oak Room), sleek Art Deco (Joseph Urban's Persian Room), postwar modernism (Henry Dreyfuss's remodeled Persian Room), faux Polynesian village (Trader Vic's), and even a Frank Lloyd Wright–furnished one-bedroom apartment (Suite 223-225).

Showcasing a variety of changing tastes in design, The Plaza has also served as a laboratory for evolving restaurant styles. There have been sixteen different on-premise dining rooms since 1907, each conceived to suit the palates of a specific decade: In the teens and twenties, the Grill Room served as the headquarters of the Lost Generation; in the thirties, the Persian Room lured café society types; in the forties, the Rendez-vous drew postwar cosmopolites. The fifties saw the birth of the Edwardian Room, a look back to the hotel's earlier days, echoing more conservative times, while the sixties welcomed Trader Vic's (one of the first theme eateries in the city) and the Oyster Bar, a nod to less formal dining. In the seventies, there was the Green Tulip, a reaction to the youthquake rocking the country, and 1994 saw the arrival of Gauguin, a restaurant-cum-discotheque that reflected the excesses of the heady eighties. The Edwardian Room lies unoccupied at the time of this writing; one can only wonder what kind of millennial statement it will make.

America's changing tastes in what constitutes a celebrity can be seen at The Plaza, as well. On opening day, captains of industry (George Jay Gould, John "Bet a Million" Gates) and men of accomplishment (Mark Twain, Enrico Caruso) were the anointed ones. By mid-century, film stars (Greta Garbo, Marilyn Monroe) and musicians (the Beatles) had usurped the place of inventors and artists as the country's idols, and as the millennium approached, supermodels, hairstylists, chefs, and florists had joined the celebrity firmament. And it seems as if all of them have visited the hotel, to dine, be married, spend the night, attend a charity event, or be honored at a testimonial dinner. There might be six degrees of separation in the rest of the world, but at The Plaza, there's but one.

The pictures in this book are arranged chronologically and recount an episodic, anecdotal history of this great hotel. Thanks to a number of serendipitous events—a prime location, visionary builders and management, and, most recently, the movies—The Plaza has become the most famous hotel in the world. That it has maintained its dignity and reputation over the century is the most remarkable thing about it.

~ Part One ~

The Site

The New York Skating Club

*O*n what would become one of New York's most fabled—and expensive—plots of land, ice-skaters once innocently frolicked. These are the earliest known photographs of The Plaza's future site, made when the land was occupied by the Fifth Avenue Pond, one of many on the undeveloped East Side of town. During the winter, this pond was reserved by the New York Skating Club for use as a private skating rink. (Below, its clubhouse around 1863; at right, the enlarged facilities around 1870.)

Ice-skating had come into vogue after the first public rink was opened in Central Park in 1858. At first, skaters were segregated by sex, as was the custom for many public activities of that era, but by 1870, this rule had been relaxed, although the female skaters at right still seem to be hovering rather timidly around the perimeter. As the cost of skates was high—ranging from thirteen dollars a pair to as much as thirty dollars—the sport had been embraced by the upper and middle classes, who built private rinks for their exclusive enjoyment. (Poorer folk made do with homemade versions constructed of wood and skated in Central Park.) Organized in 1863, the New York Skating Club was 150 members strong and was considered the most elite venue in town.

The view at right is to the north; on the other side of the roadway, now Fifty-ninth Street, lies Central Park. It all looks rather bucolic. There is no hint of what was to come, not an inkling of the wealth, the spectacle, the moments high and low that would unfold here. What would soon transpire on this modest-looking site would have surely confounded these unsuspecting skaters.

The First Plaza Hotel

$\mathcal{T}$he site did not remain a skating rink for long. Its view of Central Park and its Fifth Avenue address clearly made it one of the prime corners in the rapidly growing city, and in 1880, the land was purchased for $850,000 by a group of real estate speculators who planned to erect an apartment hotel. A loan was secured from the New York Life Insurance Company, and Carl Pfeiffer was hired as the architect and John C. Phyfe and James Campbell as the builders. Construction began in 1883, but it was doomed from the start: Phyfe and Campbell soon were over budget, and after five years of litigation, New York Life foreclosed on the half-finished building. Following more complicated financing and endless debate, the firm of McKim, Mead and White was hired to refit the uncompleted structure into a luxury hotel.

The Italian Renaissance result (at right) was finally achieved at a cost of $3 million and opened on October 1, 1890. Eight stories tall, with four hundred rooms, it was considered very fine in its day. Indeed, the line of hansom cabs parked along the entrance suggests a bustling establishment. The asphalt-lined open plaza in front of the hotel (from which it took its name) had been cut out of the city's street-grid plan for use as a carriage turnaround; there was an entrance to Central Park to the north, and it was thought that heavy traffic would necessitate such a space. As the photograph suggests, this traffic never materialized. It was not until 1916 that the area was relandscaped as a pedestrian mall, and in 1923, it was officially named Grand Army Plaza.

Below, both sides of a souvenir trade card promoting the property, given out at Chicago's 1893 World's Columbian Exposition.

The Fifth Avenue Door, Circa 1895

*A*lthough modest in comparison to the building that would follow it, the first Plaza was considered one of the city's finest hotels. Moses King's *Handbook of New York City,* a popular guide at the time, gushed over the hotel's appointments: "A large part of the main floor is finished with choice marble mosaic pavements, silvered ceilings, enfoliated bronze columns, counters of Mexican onyx, woodwork of mahogany and fine paintings. Here are the reception rooms, with their Gobelin tapestries and the great lounging rooms, where ladies and gentlemen meet amid Persian rugs, dainty tables, rich easy chairs, costly paintings and other attractive features." The hotel's symbol was the lion, and the king of the jungle was imprinted on everything from the mosaic floors to the lace curtains.

At bottom right, a view of the Fifth Avenue door, showing the main entrance facing the fashionable avenue, taken around 1895. This eastern facade featured a glass-domed entryway, Art Nouveau lanterns, and many awnings and window shades; it would be a long time before the invention of air conditioning.

Below and upper right, rare illustrations of the hotel's interior from a promotional booklet.

Fifth Avenue, 58th and 59th Streets, New York.

THE OFFICE.

LOUNGING ROOM.

RESTAURANT.

CORRIDOR, SECOND FLOOR.

TABLE D'HOTE DINING ROOM.

LADIES' PINK PARLOR.

View of Central Park from the Plaza.

At The Plaza, 1898

*T*he shot of this elegant street scene was taken from the northeast corner of the hotel, looking out onto Fifth Avenue. Like the first Plaza, none of its neighbors would remain there for long. On the left, the two buildings between Fifty-ninth and Fifty-eighth streets are the Savoy Hotel and the Balkenhayn apartment house, on the site now occupied by the General Motors Building. The handsome structure to their right was known as Marble Row, and although constructed to resemble one large residence, it was, in fact, five separate town houses. The dormered mansion partially seen at far right was the home of Cornelius Vanderbilt II, where Bergdorf Goodman stands today.

Demolition of the First Plaza Hotel

*T*he next step in the property's development came about at a luncheon in the St. Regis Hotel one afternoon in 1902. Present were the two key figures in the plan: Bernhard Beinecke, (below, left) a former meat wholesaler turned financier and Harry Black, (below, right) chairman of the U.S. Realty and Construction Company. U. S. Realty had just purchased the existing hotel for $3 million on the advice of Beinecke, the man who first envisioned a grander Plaza Hotel. Since the foundation of the existing building would not permit additional stories, Beinecke's idea was to demolish it and start from scratch.

The deal was complete after one final investor, the flamboyant John "Bet a Million" Gates, signed on. One of the richest men in the United States, Gates made his fortune by monopolizing virtually all of the patents on barbed wire; he had acquired his singular nickname due to his propensity to wager large sums of money on practically anything—most notoriously, on which raindrop on a windowpane would hit the sill first. His considerable financial resources, however, came with one stipulation—that Fred Sterry be hired as managing director of the new Plaza. Sterry, one of the most celebrated hoteliers in the country, had already been approached by Gates. "Build me my kind of hotel in New York," Sterry told him, "and I will come."

Demolition began in 1905, and soon the first Plaza (at left) was nothing more than a memory. (The neighboring Zander Institute, a Swedish exercise facility, held on until the 1920s.)

February 5, 1906

An architect was hired to plan the new hotel, an easy choice in the person of Henry Janeway Hardenbergh, a well-regarded designer of luxury apartments and hotels. Soon a steel skeleton began to rise behind a sign that announced:

> A NEW HOTEL WILL BE ERECTED ON THIS SITE AND
> OPENED IN THE FALL OF 1907
> UNDER THE MANAGEMENT OF FRED STERRY OF
> THE ROYAL POINCIANA & THE BREAKERS,
> PALM BEACH, FLA &
> THE HOMESTEAD, HOT SPRINGS, VA.

That Fred Sterry was the sole principal involved who was mentioned specifically by name was not surprising, for his name was already very familiar to upscale travelers. His career began at the United States Hotel in Saratoga Springs, New York, and at the age of twenty-seven, he was named managing director of the fashionable Homestead in Hot Springs, Virginia. This was followed by similar positions at the Royal Poinciana and the Breakers in Palm Beach, where his renown helped put the rising winter resort on the map. Sterry's exquisite taste and refined manners were the keys to his meteoric rise; his influence on every aspect of The Plaza cannot be overemphasized. (Below, his portrait.)

Opposite, The Plaza begins its ascent. In addition to the feverish construction team (which would complete the building in a record twenty-seven months), equally feverish sign painters were also at work (at bottom left). Their completed handiwork can be seen on the following pages.

The series of photos that follow depicting the building's construction were commissioned by the U.S. Realty and Construction Company. Made (and scrupulously dated) on a weekly basis, they served as a record of the hotel's progress. This was a common practice among builders at the time to protect their investments.

Architect Henry Hardenbergh's blueprint for The Plaza begins to reveal itself in this photograph taken in mid-September 1906. In keeping with the high standards that informed every aspect of this project, Hardenbergh (below) was chosen because of his peerless reputation, first made in 1884, when his Dakota Apartments went up on Central Park West. His renown was sealed with his 1891 design for the original Waldorf-Astoria, then considered the most luxurious hotel in the world. Other notable Manhattan projects included the Art Students League and the Manhattan and Martinique hotels; he also designed the Willard Hotel in Washington, D.C.

Yet this impressive body of work proved to be but a warm-up for The Plaza, universally considered Hardenbergh's masterwork. Its spectacular site offered unobstructed views of two facades of the building (a rarity in New York), and he made the most of it with a deftly articulated design that effortlessly merged a French château with a skyscraper. His work so pleased the U.S. Realty and Construction Company that he was later hired to plan another of their projects, Boston's Copley Plaza Hotel, where he repeated a number of The Plaza's design elements, including the back-to-back letters of its logo.

October 7, 1906

Though the hotel's opening was still a year off, The Plaza's facade was almost fully in place by October 1906 (opposite). Behind-the-scenes activities, meanwhile, continued at an equally rapid clip. Fred Sterry was dispatched to Europe on a massive buying trip, where he purchased Irish linen, French crystal, and Swiss lace curtains. "Building a house like this is much like making a woman's dress," he said in an interview. "Everything is specially made and specially suited for a purpose. I will venture to say there is not one stock thing in the decorations [for The Plaza]. Even the border on the mosaic floor was designed for this room, and that open circle in the bronze work was made for a clock, in turn made for that particular space, and so on with the carpets, furniture and tapestries. Quite different from the old style of opening an inn!" Quite different, indeed. Few inns boasted furniture from the Pooley Company of Philadelphia, china from L. Straus and Sons, and carpets from W. J. Sloan. Moreover, the cachet of outfitting The Plaza was not lost on its suppliers. The Pooley Company, for one, prominently featured the hotel's name in its advertising (below).

While the building had come a long way, so had the sign painters' art, with bills for a trade show, a theater, cigarettes, soap, cordials, and catsup adorning the base of the building. This would not be the last time The Plaza would serve as a backdrop for advertising promotion.

THE
PLAZA
NEW YORK

Fifth Avenue at 59th Street

THE WORLD'S
MOST LUXURIOUS HOTEL

Opened Tuesday, October 1, 1907

RATES

Single Rooms $2.50 per day, with bath $4.00, $6.00
Double Rooms with bath $6.00 to $10.00 per day.
Parlor, Bedroom and Bath $12.00 to $20.00 per day.
Parlor, two Bedrooms and two Baths $16.00, $18.00,
$20.00 and $25.00 per day.

FRED. STERRY, Managing Director

~ Part Two ~

The Legend

October 1, 1907

*T*he completed hotel cost $12.5 million, making it one of the most expensive buildings ever erected in the city, and this sum was $1 million over the original budget. The overrun came as a result of the owners' last-minute decision to acquire several neighboring brownstones along Fifty-eighth Street, in the event of future expansion. (It was a prescient investment; expansion would come a mere fourteen years later.)

There were few quibbles about the expense, however, given the stunning result, which was simplicity itself. For Hardenbergh's design was based on a column—with a clearly marked base (three stories of rusticated marble), shaft (ten stories of white glazed brick), and capital (an elaborate mansard roof). Of course, a plethora of detail enlivened the design: The shaft was softened by rounded corner turrets ending in towers, while the roof was richly ornamented with dormers and gables, lightly topped with filigree to soften its silhouette against the sky, and made from green copper and slate to echo the trees across the street in Central Park. What made it all the more grand was its size, which dwarfed all of the buildings in the neighborhood (as seen below). Time would eventually reverse this situation.

Near right, an example of the overheated press coverage that accompanied the hotel's opening.

·The Plaza·

FRED STERRY, Managing Director.

MONEY, JEWELS, AND OTHER VALUABLE PACKAGES MUST BE PLACED IN THE SAFE IN THE
OFFICE, OTHERWISE THE MANAGEMENT WILL NOT BE RESPONSIBLE FOR ANY LOSS.

ROOM	NAME	ADDRESS
	Tuesday Oct 1st 1907	
527 29 / 521 23 25 / 546	Mr & Mrs Alfred G. Vanderlip & Servant	New York
1141 43-45 / 1147	Mr & Mrs Wm G. Roelker & Maid	New York "
801-07-03	Mr. & Mrs. B. Beinecke	"
237-9-241	Mr John Young-Hepworth	Chicago
243	Master Otto Young-Hepworth	"
245	Mrs Gwendolyn Young-Hepworth	"
611-613	Mr. & Mrs. Alexander H. Revell	Chicago
615	Miss Margaret Revell	"
617	Master Alexander H. Revell Jr	"
1339-1337	Mr & Mrs Hamilton Carhartt	New York
1335-1333	Miss Carhartt	"
1104-1106	H.B. McQueen	Schenectady N.Y.
503-501-507	Mr & Mrs D.O Wickham	New York
507	Mrs Lyman H. Treadway	Cleveland. Ohio
507	Miss Elizabeth W. Treadway	do
505	Master Lyman H. Treadway Jr	do
1877	Albert Goodman	New York
335-31	Mr & Mrs Albert Lill and family	New York

Alfred Gwynne Vanderbilt Signs the Opening-Day Register

*O*ctober 1, 1907, arrived with everything at the ready, and promptly at 9:00 A.M., a carriage pulled up, bearing The Plaza's first guest. He was Alfred Gwynne Vanderbilt, the thirty-year-old millionaire sportsman, and his arrival was hardly fortuitous. Rather, it had been carefully orchestrated in advance by Fred Sterry, who wanted to send a message to the world about what kind of place The Plaza aspired to be. Vanderbilt embodied it perfectly: He was young, dashing, well known, and a scion of one of America's wealthiest families; indeed, his father owned one of the most famous dwellings in town, the sprawling mansion directly south of the hotel.

Vanderbilt's wife had been delayed by a minor automobile accident in Newport the day before (a telling detail, as most Americans had yet to experience the thrill of riding in a motorized vehicle), so he checked in alone, taking a five-room corner suite, 521–529, with a nearby room, 546, for his servant. Soon some of the smartest names in American society joined his on the register: Oliver Harriman, Col. William Jay, John Wanamaker, George Jay Gould, Cornelius K. G. Billings, Benjamin Duke, and two of the hotel's financial backers, Bernhard Beinecke and John "Bet a Million" Gates. The presence of all this wealth signaled a new style of fashionable living, one in the English manner. Rather than maintain a city home *and* a country estate (and troublesome sets of servants for each), it was now socially acceptable to keep a country estate as one's primary residence and lease a suite of apartments in a luxury hotel as one's city address.

Alfred Gwynne Vanderbilt led the way, and remained at The Plaza until 1912, when he moved to quarters in his own eponymous hotel, which had just opened on Park Avenue. Sadly, he did not have long to live, perishing on board the Cunard liner *Lusitania* after its sinking by a German U-boat in 1915.

Below, young Vanderbilt. Opposite, the first-day register.

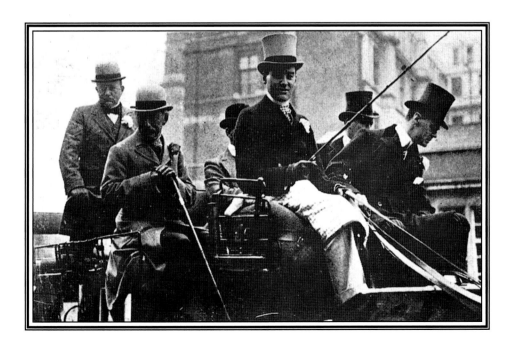

The Fifty-ninth Street Lobby

*I*t hasn't changed much over the years; today the Fifty-ninth Street lobby looks much as it did when these pictures were taken in October 1907 by photographer Joseph Byron. Byron is remembered for his portraits of high society (among his subjects were Mark Twain, Lillian Russell, and Sarah Bernhardt, as well as various Astors, Vanderbilts, and Whitneys) but is best known for his interiors, photographs of everything from millionaires' dining rooms to luxury liner lounges. He was thus the logical choice to capture The Plaza just before it opened—when it was perfection—and the splendid record he left behind (shown here and in a number of interiors immediately following) has been preserved in the archives of the Museum of the City of New York.

This was originally the hotel's sole lobby, for a vast dining room occupied what later became the Fifth Avenue entrance. Fifty-ninth Street was therefore The Plaza's nerve center, and even though the hotel was a smaller place at the time (with five hundred rooms, compared with the present eight hundred), an additional door was employed to accommodate the traffic, the portal just right of the center in the photo opposite. After the expansion of the hotel in 1921 (when the Fifth Avenue side became a lobby), this center door was eventually sealed off, refashioned into a florist shop in the forties, then remade as the concierge desk in the seventies.

Other modifications to this lobby over the years included the complete reworking of the ceiling, which was dropped to accommodate an apparatus for air conditioning, as well as the replacement of the rather primitive-looking original chandeliers with a single, more impressive model. The extravagant fixture hanging there today came courtesy of Donald and Ivana Trump, who installed it in 1989, following Trump's purchase and renovation of the property.

The Tearoom (the Palm Court)

Although Henry Hardenbergh's interior design for The Plaza was modeled after a private men's club, its centerpiece, a tearoom, had a decidedly feminine cast. A reinterpretation of the Winter Garden in London's Carlton Hotel, this vast, airy space was bordered by *fleur-de-pêche* marble columns and mirrored doors, accented with a variety of palms, and crowned by a domed yellow-and-green skylight. The room pictured at right was artfully arranged for Joseph Byron, who took this photograph just before the hotel's opening. Below, the hallway bordering it.

The builders informally referred to it as "the Lounge," guests dubbed it "the Tearoom" (which stuck), and it was not until the mid-1930s that it was formally named the Palm Court. Of all the hotel's public areas, it has been altered the most, its glass dome having been removed in 1944. This came about for a number of reasons. For one thing, the 1921 expansion of the hotel—the addition of a wing along the Fifty-eighth Street side—effectively blocked almost all of the natural light from the room, and over time the dome had fallen into bad repair and was in danger of raining debris into teacups. But more to the point, air conditioning was about to be installed, and the Palm Court's central position in the building made it a prime candidate to house the apparatus. For this combination of reasons, then, the dome was removed and replaced with a vaguely baroque ceiling. Above it, central heating and cooling units were mounted, and in the leftover space, additional rooms for private functions were fashioned.

Long a part of Plaza lore, the Palm Court has served as a setting for scenes in many popular novels and films (most notably, F. Scott Fitzgerald's *The Great Gatsby*), and, as we shall see, was the setting for its first scandal.

gram

Oct. 11, '43

oke!

Mrs. Patrick Campbell. She started a trend.

Lucius Boomer.

foremost tobacco-hater of modern times, flung himself into the fight.

Lining up his Nonsmokers Protective League, with himself as president, Dr. Pease launched his crusade to make it illegal for any woman to emulate Mrs. Patrick Campbell.

Success on Subway.

When his nonsmoking bill came before the Board of Aldermen the good doctor threw in a joker, making it illegal for a man to smoke in a woman's presence. After much debate the bill failed.

Searching for new targets, the doctor focused his fire on the subways, which had been running then for three or four years. Every time he paid his nickel for a subway ride, the doctor complained he risked death by suffocation. So he fought on for smokeless subways.

This time he won. A year or so after Mrs. Campbell's puff a the Plaza tobacco smoking wa banned by law in the subways and that's the way it's been eve since.

Dr. Pease died recently at 84 reputably the greatest enemy to bacco ever had. However, Jerom Brooks, the New Yorker who ha finished a four-volume encyclopedia on tobacco, says that Dr Pease was almost broadminded.

"Modern smokers," Mr. Brook advises, "have never encountered anything like old Shah Abbas of Persia."

When the Shah wasn't toastin tobacco venders on their own to

brated glare, inhaled with unconcern and nonchalantly blew a smoke ring at the offender's eye.

"My dear fellow," she said, icily, "I have been given to understand this is a free country. I intend to do nothing to alter its status."

The waiter fluttered back to Mr. Boomer, who was watching the action from a strategic distance.

Meanwhile, Mrs. Campbell's cigaret went out. The lady, flicking a contemptuous ash, rose from her table and slowly walked across the room to the door.

The next day New York was astir.

Mrs. Clinton B. Fisk, president of the Home Missionary Society, issued the first communique from her W. 58th St. drawing room.

"I hope I shall never see the

tell her she embarrasses the management."

The waiter threw up his arms helplessly. "I do," he cried, "she only laugh."

But he obediently ventured back to the great lady's table.

"Madame,' he implored, almost in tears, "Madame, please stop, please."

A Free Country.

Mrs. Patrick Campbell Lights a Cigarette

*T*he Plaza had been open barely a month when scandal made an early appearance with the arrival of Mrs. Patrick Campbell on November 15, 1907. A star of the British stage, the unconventional Mrs. Campbell was known to her fans as "Mrs. Pat" and the "English Sarah Bernhardt"; she had also gained renown because of a great friendship with playwright George Bernard Shaw (who later wrote *Pygmalion* for her). Stopping at The Plaza for the first leg of an American tour, Mrs. Pat had come to perform in *Hedda Gabler* and several other plays. (At right, a *carte de visite* showing the actress in costume for the role.)

She arrived with her dog, a monkey griffon named Pinkie Panky Poo, and immediately established a precedent: Management decided on the spot to admit animals to the hotel, a policy in place to this day. Once ensconced in her Plaza suite, Mrs. Pat allowed the press up for an interview, where she held forth on a variety of topics. Afterward, she decided to go downstairs for dinner.

The consequences of this decision would be loudly debated in newspapers across the country in the days to follow. For Mrs. Pat, after ordering her dinner, reached into her bag, extracted a perfumed Egyptian cigarette, and lit it. She then proceeded to smoke it—in public. In an age when such a thing was unthought of, this provocative act did not go unchallenged: The headwaiter appeared instantly and insisted that the cigarette be put out. "My good man," Mrs. Pat legendarily replied. "I understand this is a free country. I shall do nothing to change it."

A compromise of sorts was effected: A screen was brought so that the sight of her cigarette would not offend the other diners. Somehow, the press got wind of the story, and a great debate began over the evils of smoking (regardless of gender). Several years later, as part of this crusade, New York City banned smoking on its subways, a law said to have come about as a result of Mrs. Pat's folly.

Opposite, a 1940s news clipping recounting the scandal.

The Men's Cafe (the Edwardian Room)

*L*ocated on the prime northeast corner of the property, the Men's Cafe offered prized views of both Central Park and Fifth Avenue in a Spanish Renaissance setting, complete with a beamed ceiling, tile floors, wood paneling, and sturdy furniture. Exclusively a male domain, it was home to an early version of what was later called the "power breakfast," although the typical menu—pig knuckles and mutton chops—and the players—Mark Twain and Diamond Jim Brady—have changed over the years. As none of the hotel's restaurants had been given formal names, the room was offhandedly referred to as "the Cafe."

It did not remain a male domain for long. In 1920, following a shuffling of restaurant space brought about by Prohibition and an expansion of the property, the Cafe admitted ladies and became the hotel's principal dining room. Still without a name, it was finally dubbed the Plaza Restaurant in the early forties, and remained so until 1955, when it was named the Edwardian Room in honor of the age that it personifies. In 1971, a disastrous experiment transformed it into a trendy boîte called the Green Tulip, featuring hanging plants and faux Tiffany lamps. This incarnation proved mercifully short-lived, and the room resumed its former name and atmosphere in 1974. It has been used as a space for private functions since 1998.

The Men's Bar (the Oak Room)

*O*f all the public rooms in The Plaza, the Men's Bar was said to be architect Henry Hardenbergh's favorite. A German Renaissance tour de force, the oak-paneled room looks virtually the same today as it does in Joseph Byron's 1907 photograph at right. The only difference is the bar itself (running between the columns in the rear), which was removed in 1920 to comply with the new law of Prohibition. Otherwise, all of Hardenbergh's design touches remain in this architectural ode to the pleasures of drinking: the frescoes of Bavarian castles, the faux wine casks carved into the woodwork, the coats of arms set into the moldings, and the grape-laden chandelier, topped by a barmaid hoisting a stein. (The tapestries currently hanging on the walls were added by Donald and Ivana Trump in 1989.)

Originally a male sanctuary, it was informally dubbed "the Barroom" and, for a short period, boasted a burbling electric fountain as its centerpiece (below). For the duration of Prohibition, it was used for storage, then reopened as a dining room and officially named the Oak Room around 1934. Although ladies were then admitted for dinner, it remained a male domain at lunchtime until 1969.

The Plaza Crest

The back-to-back *P*'s that comprise The Plaza's crest, embedded in everything from cornices to bath towels, have long intrigued the hotel's guests, yet the origins of this symbol are somewhat hazy. It most certainly came from architect Henry Hardenbergh's office, for the same design was used in the hotel he built in Boston, the Copley Plaza. (A common explanation for the "meaning" of The Plaza's crest is that the double *P*'s symbolize the proximity of Central *P*ark and Grand Army *P*laza, but the Copley Plaza disproves this premise: It does not have a park and plaza side by side.)

More likely is the theory suggested by architecture critic Paul Goldberger. Private men's clubs were all the rage at the turn of the century, and they generally identified themselves with elaborate monograms fashioned from their initials. These monograms were displayed on flags hanging outside the clubs, which usually bore no other identifying sign.

Since Hardenbergh built a hotel that conveyed the feeling of a private club—and never included a sign with the hotel's name anywhere on the facade—he no doubt followed the custom of designing a monogram for it. Making a symmetrical design out of the top-heavy letter *P* was a challenge, but Hardenbergh followed the lead of French builders, who often placed letters backward in their designs. As he was creating a French Renaissance structure, this choice was particularly apt, and memorable.

The Dining Room (the Fifth Avenue Lobby)

*O*pposite the Tearoom lay The Plaza's main Dining Room (site of the Fifth Avenue lobby today), one vast space that also included what was later known as the Rose Room. This dining room welcomed both sexes, although it was segregated into two sections, separated by movable glass partitions—one reserved for the hotel's permanent guests, the other for transients and visitors. Considered most choice (and naturally held for permanent guests) was the south side of the room, which overlooked Fifty-eighth Street; apparently, the food was even more delicious when eaten while looking at the splendid Cornelius Vanderbilt mansion across the street.

Opposite, the dining room, done in shades of rose, whose windows overlooked Fifth Avenue. This page, the opposite view, as seen from Fifth Avenue. Very early on, a seasonal outdoor restaurant named the Champagne Porch was fashioned in the narrow forty-by-fifteen-foot space between the columns and the building proper. With only ten tables, the Porch was the most exclusive dining experience in the hotel, patronized by the likes of Diamond Jim Brady and the Prince of Wales. Its prices were equally celestial, with champagne running from ten to fifteen dollars a bottle, and a complete dinner approaching the then-astronomical sum of fifty dollars.

The Porch closed after the Volstead Act became law. The dining room itself was dismantled and converted into a lobby in 1921, concurrent with the addition of an annex to the building along the Fifty-eighth Street side.

Luncheon Menu, July 4, 1911

*A*menu for an Independence Day luncheon in the main dining room. It was also rendered on the reverse in French (not shown), as was the style of the time.

The Plaza

-: *Luncheon* :-

Cape Cods 30   Blue Points 30   Cherry Stone Clams 35
Crab Flake Cocktail 50   Lobster Cocktail 60   Clam Cocktail 40
Little Neck Clams 30 Crab Flake Suprême 75 Fresh Astrakan Caviar, p. p. 1 00
Smoked salmon 50   Antipasto 60   Carciofini 75   Salami 40
Smoked sterlet 50 Hors d'Oeuvres, Frivole, p. p. 50 Senfgurken 30 Celery 50
Mortadella, p. p. 30   Kieler Sprotten, p. p. 30

SOUPS

Petite marmite 60 35   Consommé 50 30   Chicken consommé 60 35
Chicken Home made 60 35   Consommé fumet of tomatoes 60 35   Santé 50 30
Washington 60 35   Purée St. Germain 50 30   Chicken gumbo 60 35
Julienne 50 30   Tomato 50 30

FISH
(English sole and turbotin to order (whole)

Baked chicken halibut with salt pork 90 50   Brook trout sautée Meunière 60
Broiled Lake bass, mustard sauce 90 50   Filet of kingfish, Choisy 90 50
Cassolette of lobster, American style p. p. 60   English sole, Héloise 1 50
Gougeonnette of flounder, tartar sauce 80 45   Cold salmon, Parisian p. p. 50
Soft shell crabs sautés Newburg (2) 50   Cold lobster, Belle-Vue p. p. 80

Cold egg, Martha (1) 40   Cold egg with ham (1) 40   Shirred eggs, Meyerbeer 60
Poached eggs, Grand Duc 60   Egg in cocotte Edison (1) 30

ENTREES

Roast beef, potatoes fondantes 1 00 60   Calf's brains, brown butter 90 50
Sauté of chicken, Ambassadrice 1 25 70   Lamb trotters, Poulette 90 50
Leg of lamb, Lima beans Forestière 1 00 60   Minced chicken, Sterry 1 50 80
Tenderloin of pork sauté with apples 90 50   Broiled squab, Signora 1 25
Veal chop, fine herbs, spinach English style 80 Sirloin steak, marrow Bordelaise 1 50

ROASTS

Roast lamb 1 00 60   Rib of Beef 75 40 extra cut 1 25 70   Squab Chicken 1 25
Poularde du Mans 5.00   Duckling Rouennais 5.00   Chicken Reine 3.50
Chicken 2 50 1 50   Broiled chicken 2 00 1 00

COLD MEATS

Terrine of Guinea hen, p. pers. 60   Boneless squab, Véronique or Richelieu 1 50
Suprême of chicken Plaza (1) 1 25   Chicken and ham pie p. p. 60
Lamb 1 00 60   Assorted meat 90   Galantine of capon, truffed p. p. 60
Corned beef 50   Lobster 1 25   Virginia ham 75
Smoked beef tongue 50   Squab with jelly 1 25

VEGETABLES

Potatoes:- Champs Elysée 50   O'Brien 40   Delmonico 40
New asparagus, p. pers. 60   New Lima beans 75   New corn 60
Cauliflower au gratin 60 35   Fried egg plant 50 30   Corn fritters 35
Argenteuil asparagus 1 25   New peas 75   Oyster Bay asparagus 90 50
New string beans 75   Cardon with marrow 60
French peas 60 35   French artichoke, Hollandaise sauce 60
Celery with gravy 60   Cêpes Bordelaise 75

SALADS

            Saratoga 75 40   Louise 75 40
Lobster 1 25 70   Panachée 60 35   Chiffonnade 75   Chicken 1 00 60
Cucumber 50 30   Tomato 50 30   Lettuce 50 30   Romaine 60 35

SWEETS

Mirlitons de Rouen 25   Independence pudding 35
Savarin with cream 30   Berliner fritters 35
Assorted cakes 10 each   Chocolate éclairs 10 each   Petits fours 30

ICE CREAM

Raspberry sherbet 40   Coffee mousse 40   Fancy ice cream 30
Vanilla 30   Lemon 30   Chocolate 30   Tutti frutti 40   Biscuit Tortoni 40
Fresh Strawberry 40   Vanilla basket with strawberries 50   Raspberry 30
                Fresh peach 40

CHEESE

Neufchatel 30   Stilton 30
Camembert 30   Cream 30   Gorgonzola 30   Imported Brie 30
Port du Salut 30   Roquefort 30   Vermont sage cheese 25

FRUITS

Sliced peaches and cream p. p. 50   Hot house grapes, white or black 1 50
Blackberries, Raspberries, Blueberries, Strawberries p. pers. 40   Peaches 75 40
Hot House Melon, p.p. 75   Cantaloupe 75 40   Watermelon, p.p. 50
Grape fruit Suprême 75   Grape fruit 75 40   Cherries 75 40
Pear 20   Apple 20   Orange 20   Assorted fruit 1 00
        Coffee with milk 25   Demi-tasse 15
        HALF PORTION SERVED TO ONE PERSON ONLY.
                Tuesday, July 4th 1911

The Ballroom

*S*ociety first patronized hotel ballrooms for parties and benefits following the Civil War, and by the turn of the century, no hotel of any consequence was without one. By the time The Plaza opened in 1907, amateur theatricals and tableaux vivants had become popular amusements among the upper classes, and so ballroom stages were also de rigueur. The Plaza's stage was a mechanical marvel, a forty-five-by-eight-foot structure manufactured by the Otis Elevator Company that could be transformed by the press of a button into a balcony when not in use. This stage would descend quite memorably on January 24, 1908, for a single performance of *Mrs. Van Vechten's Divorce Dance,* a one-act play that was the social event of the season, as its star was Mrs. George Jay Gould—former showgirl turned society figure and Plaza resident. (At right, Mr. and Mrs. Gould pose in the bedroom of their suite.)

The Ballroom was witness to many gala events, beginning with the first formal dinner held there (below), a fifteen-dollar-a-plate, ten-course affair thrown by the Pilgrims of America in honor of the Lord Bishop of London. The Lord Bishop had recently beaten President Theodore Roosevelt in a game of tennis, and he got a laugh from the crowd when he crowed about it during his after-dinner remarks.

This original Ballroom was situated on the northwest corner of the building, just above the Oak Room, and soon proved to be too small for the burgeoning social scene. When The Plaza expanded in 1921, a larger version was constructed as part of the Fifty-eighth Street addition. The original model was eventually subdivided into two separate floors, which today house the Baroque Room and, above it, the general manager's office.

Nº I Mr. Mrs. George Say Gould
in Hotel plaza.

INAUGURATION OF

Motor Cab Service

NEW YORK TAXICAB CO.

TARIFF:

1 to 4 Passengers, Day or Night Service

First half-mile or fraction thereof - - -	Thirty Cents
Each quarter-mile thereafter - - -	Ten Cents
Each six minutes of waiting - - -	Ten Cents

The service will start to-day at the following six places:

New Plaza Hotel   New Netherland Hotel   St. Regis Hot e
Knickerbocker Hotel   Rector's Restaurant
Imperial Hotel

Siz Hundred Taxicabs will shortly be in service. Additional stands will be established at most of the hotels, restaurants and clubs.

All Taxicabs are bright red, with green panel. Uniformed drivers. Four-cylinder French cars—open or closed. **LOOK FOR THE COLOR.**

TELEPHONE 4873 BRYANT

HARRY N. ALLEN, *Pres. and Gen. Mgr.*

546 Fifth Avenue, New York

(Silo Building)

The Plaza and the Taxicab

*N*ew York's first motorized taxi fleet made its debut on city streets the same day The Plaza did—October 1, 1907—a date most carefully selected by the fleet's owner, Harry Allen, to take full advantage of the hotel's coattails. With much fanfare, Allen's twenty-five-car fleet was paraded up Fifth Avenue to The Plaza, where the taxis were parked around the perimeter. Photographs were taken (opposite and below) and Plaza patrons were given free rides for the day.

Allen's "auto-cars"—painted red and sporting a green stripe for easy identification—were driven by chauffeurs dressed like hussars and came equipped with a revolutionary "taximeter," a device that allowed riders to monitor the progress of their fare. At first, drivers of hansom cabs dismissed their motorized competition as a novelty that would soon pass, but the taxicab's growing success soon made them uneasy. Tempers flared, reaching their peak one morning in the winter of 1909, when Allen was having breakfast in the Men's Cafe at The Plaza. Shots rang out from the park, shattering a window but fortunately missing their target. Though the gunman was never apprehended, Allen got the message. He sold his business, which then numbered over six hundred cars.

The hansom cabs faded away to a mere handful, hanging on only as a quaint tourist attraction and limited to travel through Central Park. Ironically enough, one of the few sites where they can still be hailed is at The Plaza, where their demise was first foreseen.

Bottom left, an advertisement for the fleet from a hotel trade journal.

The Cornelius Vanderbilt Mansion

*D*irectly south of The Plaza stood the mansion of Cornelius Vanderbilt II, grandson of the famed Commodore Vanderbilt, the patriarch of this spectacularly wealthy family. Modeled loosely after the French Château du Blois, the blockwide home lay along the Fifth Avenue corridor known as Vanderbilt Row, and it went up in two stages: The initial dwelling facing Fifty-seventh Street was completed in 1882, followed by the addition of a carriage entrance in 1892 along Fifty-eighth Street (shown at right). This huge house employed thirty servants, whose main occupation seemed to be keeping it dust-free. Vanderbilt's sentiments about the arrival of The Plaza are unrecorded, but he must have given some tacit approval, as his son Alfred was the hotel's first guest.

The mansion was demolished in 1927 and replaced by the Bergdorf Goodman department store. Among items salvaged from it were an elaborate marble fireplace (today part of the collection of the Metropolitan Museum of Art) and the iron gates shown here, which were transplanted uptown to the city's Conservatory Gardens.

Below, a circa 1910 view, looking up Fifth Avenue and showing the Fifty-seventh Street facade of the mansion (left of center) with The Plaza looming behind it.

The Sherman Monument

For nearly a century, the equestrian statue of the Civil War's renowned Gen. William Tecumseh Sherman has stood guard over the plaza in front of the hotel. Dedicated on May 30, 1903, it is the second-oldest structure extant in this neighborhood (preceded only by the Metropolitan Club of 1894), and among the most well-regarded works of Augustus Saint-Gaudens, one of America's leading sculptors at the time. *William Tecumseh Sherman,* as the work is titled, had been in progress since 1888 (when Sherman himself posed for the head) and was completed in 1903. The finished work depicts the Union army hero being led into battle by Victory, personified by a young woman bearing a palm branch; its polished granite pedestal was designed by Charles McKim of the noted New York architectural firm McKim, Mead and White.

Sherman's monument was originally intended to be placed in front of Grant's Tomb, but Grant's family objected, not wanting his grave to be upstaged by another general. A Times Square site was discussed and rejected, while Saint-Gaudens himself prevailed for a park setting—and finally got one on the southeast corner of Central Park. At the artist's direction, the bronze figure was given a coat of gold leaf, which quickly eroded (as it appears to have already done in the photo at right, though it is more apparent in the postcard below). When the gilding was reapplied in the late 1980s, a great hue and cry arose over the statue's glitzy new look, yet this was Saint-Gaudens's intention: He was "sick of seeing statues look like stovepipes."

In 1916, the monument was integrated into the design of Grand Army Plaza and moved sixteen feet west to align it with the newly constructed Pulitzer Fountain.

7242. WILLIAM T. SHERMAN STATUE, CENTRAL PARK, NEW YORK. ORIGINAL COPYRIGHT, 1903, BY AUGUSTUS SAINT GAUDENS. THIS CARD AUTHORIZED

Enrico Caruso and the Magneta Clock

*T*he famed tenor was an early guest at The Plaza, arriving in November 1907 for his fourth consecutive season as a performer at the Metropolitan Opera. Caruso arrived with some trepidation, however, for his visit to the United States the previous year had been marked by two calamities: First, he had been caught in the nightmare of the San Francisco earthquake, and then, even worse, he was arrested in New York's Central Park Zoo for allegedly pinching a woman in the monkey house. The charges had been dismissed after Caruso paid a ten-dollar fine, and his greatest fear—not being allowed back into the country the following season—proved groundless.

He had no doubt chosen to stop at The Plaza because it was the talk of the town, having been open only one month at this point and much touted for its lavishness. His corner suite, although traditionally appointed, was subtly up-to-date, with a telephone in every room, buzzers that summoned maids and waiters, and a Magneta clock on the fireplace mantel. Considered a state-of-the-art instrument at the time, the Magneta was known for its absolute accuracy, as all the clocks were wired to a master unit in the telephone room. The price of this precision was a low hum, unheard by the average ear.

Caruso did not have the average ear, however, and on December 8, all 245 of the Magneta clocks in the house stopped simultaneously when he attacked the one in his room with a knife (some accounts suggest a shoe or a suitcase as his weapon) in order to silence it. Management's reaction was swift: They sent Caruso a magnum of champagne and a letter of apology; "accidents" were handled differently in those days. These tokens apparently did little good, for when Caruso returned to the city the following season, he took up residence at the Knickerbocker Hotel, which he patronized for the next twelve years.

The souvenir booklet illustration opposite depicts the singer as Canio in *I Pagliacci,* his most famous role. The Magneta clock advertisement (below) comes from the trade journal *Hotel Review.*

SPECIMEN OF CLOCK MANTEL SETS INSTALLED BY US THROUGHOUT THE NEW

PLAZA HOTEL

No Batteries or Contact-Points Employed

The Most Up-to-date Electric Time Clock System on the Market

Contracts Recently Secured Include:

The new 42-story Singer Building, N. Y. The New Union Depot, Washington, D. C.
The New York "Staats Zeitung" Building The Cunard Liner S. S. "Lusitania"
The St. Francis Hotel, San Francisco, Etc.

The Magneta Co., 120-122 W. 31st St., N. Y.

New Plaza Hotel.

The Plaza Hotel, New York

Hotel Plaza, New York City

Plaza Hotel, opposite Central Park
at 59th Street, New York City.

5188. The Plaza Hotel, New York.

The Postcard Craze and The Plaza

A mania for collecting and sending picture postcards swept America in the first decade of the twentieth century, taking The Plaza along with it. The craze was some time in coming. The first (pictureless) government-issued postcards were introduced in 1873, followed by cards illustrated with scenes from the World's Columbian Exposition of 1893, yet the populace took little notice. It was not until the passing of the Private Mailing Card Act of 1898—which gave private manufacturers the right to publish and sell their own cards—that the floodgates opened. Postcards took the country by storm, with the fad reaching its peak by 1908, when nearly 700 million postcards were mailed in the United States (whose population at the time was about 89 million). By far the most popular subjects were scenic views, and in New York City, The Plaza was much depicted, being a grand new source of civic pride.

Most postcards were printed in Germany, which virtually monopolized the market due to its superior printing techniques. Plates were made from black-and-white photographs that were then hand-colored by German artisans, who had never actually seen their subjects, which explains the varying hues of the hotel illustrated here. Many cards also titled the hotel the "New Plaza" to differentiate it from its predecessor.

The postcard craze abated around the time of World War I, diminished by the abrupt unavailability of German printers and also by the introduction of the folded greeting card in 1913. Many of the turn-of-the-century postcards that survive today were never sent, proof that they were just as collectible then as now.

THE NEW PLAZA HOTEL, NEW YORK

Hotel Plaza, Fifth Avenue & 59th Street, New York.
Series 1295 A.   Davidson Brother

Princess Lwoff-Parlaghy Adopts a Pet

One of The Plaza's more eccentric guests, Princess Vilma Lwoff-Parlaghy, registered in 1908. Although history has forgotten her, the princess was quite a well-known figure of that era. Her title (and fortune) had been acquired after a brief marriage to a Russian prince, but she was famed as an accomplished portraitist, whose subjects included many of the crowned heads of Europe. In addition, she was also an early champion of animal rights, maintaining a menagerie in her château in the south of France. She had come to the United States to paint the country's leading public figures, and originally planned to encamp at the Waldorf-Astoria, but was turned away. They did not allow pets. Instead, she took an expansive suite of rooms at the more animal-friendly Plaza, where, along with her pets, she was accompanied by a retinue that included a physician, several bodyguards, and a father confessor. To everyone's surprise, she stayed for nearly five years.

And her stay was not without incident. Soon after her arrival, the princess fell in love with a lion cub she spotted at the Ringling Brothers circus; she tried to buy it but was rebuffed. Determined to have it, she came up with a plan: One of her recent portraits depicted Civil War hero Gen. Daniel E. Sickles (also a figure of some renown at the time), and she convinced him to ask Ringling Brothers for the cub, knowing they would not refuse him. Her scheme worked, and Sickles, in turn, gave her the animal, which was named in his honor, although nicknamed "Goldfleck." Somehow, Fred Sterry, The Plaza's managing director, was persuaded to allow Goldfleck his own room in the hotel, although with a round-the-clock trainer close by. Inevitably, the cub managed to escape from his room one afternoon, and he roamed the hallways until he was coaxed back inside by some irresistible bait, a hunk of raw meat.

Hotel living apparently didn't suit Goldfleck, and the animal took sick and died in 1912. The princess was heartbroken, and after a private funeral ceremony in her quarters, Goldfleck was buried in the animal cemetery in Hartsdale, New York, where his tombstone (at left) remains something of an attraction today. The princess (at right) suffered a reversal of fortune at the onset of World War I and eventually relinquished her Plaza suite for more modest quarters on East Thirty-ninth Street, where she died in 1923.

The Plaza Lighted for the Hudson-Fulton Celebration

A glorious burst of civic pride, the Hudson-Fulton Celebration captivated New Yorkers over a two-week period, which began on September 25, 1909. Although the festivities ostensibly honored two significant marine events—Henry Hudson's discovery of the Hudson River in 1609 and Robert Fulton's steamboat trip up the river in 1807—they really seemed an excuse to let off some patriotic steam.

The city pulled out all the stops. Innumerable dinners, elaborate parades, special art exhibits, and nightly fireworks thrilled the populace. An armada of eight hundred vessels from around the world conducted maneuvers in the harbor. Wilbur Wright brought his aeroplane to New York and made the first flight over Manhattan, from Governors Island to Grant's Tomb and back again. But most stirring for the general public was the illumination of the city, turning New York into Coney Island. (Electric light was still enough of a novelty at the time to be wondrous.) Bridges, public monuments, and many private buildings joined together to create a "City of Light."

The Plaza was among them, and its illumination was dazzling, even if some of the lights in the photographs shown here appear to be courtesy of a retoucher. The hotel itself was the center of much activity: It was host to the official representatives of the Netherlands (whose gift to the city was a full-size replica of Hudson's ship, the *Half Moon*), and it had its own reviewing stand for parade watchers, constructed on the hotel's northeast corner.

Below, the northern facade illuminated in a photograph by Jessie Tarbox Beals, the first female photojounalist. Beals's picture is the only record of The Plaza bearing a sign with its name in electric lights (along the roofline).

The Pulitzer Fountain

What to do about the undeveloped asphalt-lined open area in front of The Plaza had been a topic of debate among municipal planners as early as 1898, but it was not until the 1911 death of newspaper publisher Joseph Pulitzer that a formal design took shape. Pulitzer had bequeathed fifty thousand dollars to the city "for the erection of a fountain . . . preferably at or near the Plaza entrance at 59th Street. . . ." Proponents of the City Beautiful movement (which espoused grand civic architecture in public spaces for the ennoblement of the populace) suggested a fully redesigned space to accommodate it, loosely based on the Place de la Concorde in Paris. A competition was held and won by Thomas Hastings, of the architectural firm Carrère and Hastings, whose final plan closely adhered to the City Beautiful model: two semicircular islands, anchored on one end by Saint-Gaudens's Sherman Monument and by the fountain on the other.

Work began in 1914 with the realignment of the Sherman Monument so that it would fit into the overall symmetric design. Austrian sculptor Karl Bitter was commissioned to fashion an allegorical female figure to top the fountain, and he began work on a statue of Pomona, Roman goddess of abundance, but died just after completing a two-foot model; the final work, executed in bronze and titled *Abundance,* was finished by two of his assistants, Karl Gruppe and Isidore Konti, and officially dedicated in May 1916.

Below, an engineer inspects the project's progress. At right, the completed fountain, surrounded by balustrades and Doric columns, which were later removed during a renovation in the 1930s.

Pulitzer Fountain. Plaza 5th Ave and 58 St. C11807
Copyright 1916 by Irving Underhill

versary, or an important thing that I should do.
But it hid itself persistently in the overpowering
heat.
  "Come on over!" called Daisy. "Everybody's got
to help decide. Tom says I haven't any common
sense."
  We went over to the car.
  "The nearest place is the Plaza," she continued
facetiously. "We can take a room there and go to
sleep. Or else we could engage five tiled bathrooms
and take cold baths."
  Tom was thoughtful for a moment.
  "I'll tell you," he said, "we'll get a room there
and have a mint julep and talk it over."
  "Talk what over?" asked Daisy uneasily.
  "What we're going to do." And he added casually:
"Or whatever's on your mind."
  "But I don't want to take a room. I think it's
the silliest thing I ever——"
  "Whether you want to or not, that's what we're
going to do," he interrupted grimly.
  Gatsby looked questioningly at Daisy.
  "If you don't want to——"
  "She wants to," said Tom. "And I'm quite able
to talk to her myself."

B.Galley 39
  "The thing to do is to forget about the heat", said Tom im-
patiently, "You make it ten times worse by crabbing about it."
  He unrolled the bottle of whiskey from the towel and put it
on the table.
  "Why not let her alone, old sport," remarked Gatsby, "You're the one
that wanted to come to town."
  There was a moment of silence. The telephone book slipped
from its nail and splashed to the floor, whereupon Jordan whispered
"Excuse me" -- but this time no one laughed.
  "I'll pick it up", I offered.
  "I've got it, old sport", Gatsby examined the parted string,
muttered "Hum!" in an interested way, and tossed the book on a chair.
  "That's a great expression of yours, isn't it?" said Tom sharply.
  "What is?"
  "All this 'old sport' business. Where'd you pick that up?"
  "Now see here, Tom", said Daisy, turning around from the mirror,
"if you're going to make personal remarks I won't stay here a minute.
Call up and order some ice for the mint julep."
  As Tom took up the receiver the compressed heat exploded into
sound and we were listening to the portentous chords of Mendelssohn's
Wedding March from the ballroom below.
  "Imagine marrying anybody in this heat!" cried Jordan dismally.
  "Still -- I was married in the middle of June", Daisy remembered,
"Louisville in June! Somebody fainted. Who was it fainted, Tom?"
  "Biloxi", he answered shortly.
  "A man named Biloxi. 'Blocks' Biloxi, and he made boxes -- that's
a fact -- and he was from Biloxi, Tennessee."
  "They carried him into my house", appended Jordan, "because we
lived just two doors from the church. And he stayed three weeks,
until Daddy told him he had to get out. The day after he left
Daddy died." After a moment she added, "There wasn't any connection".
  "I used to know a Bill Biloxi from Memphis", I remarked.
  "That was his cousin. I knew his whole family history before he
left. He gave me an alluminium putter that I use today."
  Gatsby and Tom took no part in this conversation, I don't think
either of them moved but I had the impression, somehow, that they
were both walking rapidly round and round the room. The music had
died down as the ceremony began and now a long cheer floated in at
the window, followed by intermittent cries of "Yea - ea - ea!" and
finally by a burst of jazz as the dancing began.
  "We're getting old", said Daisy, "If we were young we'd rise
and dance."
  "Remember Biloxi", Jordan warned her, "Where'd you know him,
Tom?"
  "Biloxi?" He concentrated with an effort, "I didn't know him.
He was a friend of Daisy's."
  "He was not", she denied. "I'd never seen him before. He came
down in the private car."
  "Well, he said he knew you. He said he was raised in Louisville.
Asa Bird brought him around at the last minute and asked if we had
room for him."
  Jordan smiled.

F. Scott Fitzgerald and *The Great Gatsby*

*T*he Plaza has long been an inspiration for writers, and among the first was novelist F. Scott Fitzgerald, the golden boy of 1920s literature. Fitzgerald and his wife, Zelda, led much-publicized madcap lives and were ardent Plaza patrons, frequenting the Grill Room, the hotel's least formal basement restaurant. Not long after the Fitzgeralds' 1920 marriage, the newlyweds moved into an apartment at 38 West Fifty-ninth Street, just doors down from the Grill. During this period, they made nightly appearances there and one evening Fitzgerald frolicked—cold sober—in the Pulitzer Fountain in front of the hotel. Unfortunately, photographs of this notorious misadventure were never made; the portrait of Scott and Zelda (below, right) was taken somewhere in Alabama in the summer of 1920 and was later used to illustrate a magazine piece called "The Cruise of the Rolling Junk."

Like most novelists, Fitzgerald incorporated his own experiences into his work, and thus The Plaza appeared frequently as a setting in his novels and short stories. *The Beautiful and Damned,* his second novel, featured scenes set in the Grill Room, and his masterpiece, *The Great Gatsby,* used the Tearoom and a guest room as backgrounds. (Opposite, Fitzgerald's galley proofs for the climactic scene in The Plaza suite in *The Great Gatsby;* below left, the book's original dust jacket.)

Fitzgerald's passion for The Plaza was famously reflected in a letter written to the author by his friend Ernest Hemingway. "If you really feel blue enough, get yourself heavily insured and I'll see you can get killed," Hemingway joked, "and I'll write you a fine obituary . . . and we can take your liver out and give it to the Princeton Museum, [and] your heart to the Plaza Hotel."

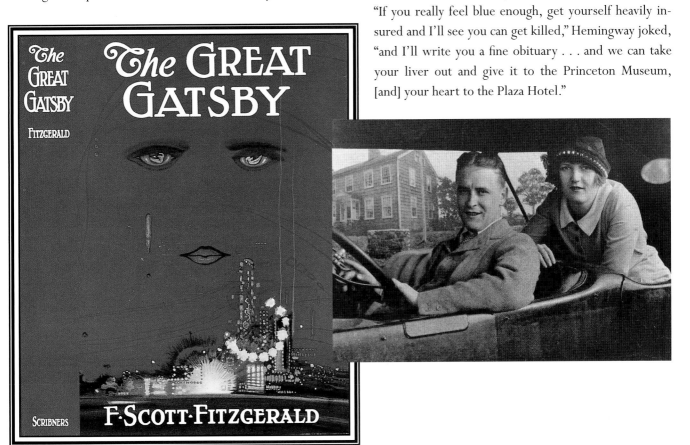

CADILLAC SHOWS THE WORLD

..*how truly magnificent a motor car can be !*

CADILLAC-FLEETWOOD *Series 75 Five-Passenger Formal Sedan, $3685*. Six-wheel equipment with fender wells, tire cover, wheel discs, license frames and white sidewall tires optional at extra cost.*

Those who desire the utmost in mechanical excellence and distinction will find these qualities carried to new heights in the Cadillac-Fleetwood creations for 1937. And as the motoring world discovers that Cadillac-Fleetwood prices begin at $2595*, the decided preference for Cadillac in the fine car field will become even more pronounced.

Now available in thirteen Bodies by Fleetwood.   Individual custom designs prepared on request

THE NEW CADILLAC·FLEETWOOD V 8·12·16

FROM THE ROYAL FAMILY OF MOTORDOM

*Delivered Price at Detroit, Michigan: $2595 and up, subject to change without notice. This price includes all standard accessories. Transportation, State and Local Taxes, Optional Accessories and Equipment—Extra.

New York, 1930

*N*ot even The Plaza was immune to America's Great Depression. Business was down, to say the least, but a more significant and enduring change came about as the hotel's sprawling suites were vacated one by one. The vogue for permanent residence in luxury hotels was over, toppled by changing tastes and reversals of fortune. After the addition of a wing along the Fifty-eighth Street side in 1921—adding rooms, as opposed to suites—The Plaza became a much more transient hotel than it had been in Alfred Gwynne Vanderbilt's day.

Despite hard times, optimism ran unchecked in the hyperbolic world of advertising, a thriving institution that had come into its own in the 1920s. Opposite, a 1937 Cadillac ad depicting Grand Army Plaza as seen from the Fifth Avenue door (the hotel crest is visible on the marquee at upper left). The illustration suggests the perfect world that exists only in advertisements: There might be a depression on, but cars were huge, and well-off Plaza patrons always could be counted on to have a nickel for the newsboy.

Below, a quintessential view of 1930s New York as seen from Central Park, showing the Pierre, Sherry-Netherland, and Savoy-Plaza hotels, the Squibb Building and The Plaza.

The Persian Room

*T*his legendary nightclub opened on April 1, 1934—four months after the repeal of Prohibition—and was quickly a favorite haunt of café society. Formerly the southern half of the Fifth Avenue dining room, the space had been reinterpreted in streamlined Art Deco by the Viennese designer Joseph Urban. Urban was both a stage designer and architect, responsible for everything from the sets of the *Ziegfeld Follies* to the design of the New School in Greenwich Village. The Persian Room proved to be one of his last commissions; he died shortly before its opening.

Over its forty-one-year run, the nightclub showcased an impressive array of talent. The opening act—Tony and Renee De-Marco (below)—were veterans of the exhibition dancing circuit, a popular nightclub entertainment since the days of Vernon and Irene Castle, which enjoyed renewed popularity in the thirties largely due to the success of Fred Astaire and Ginger Rogers. The DeMarcos made a career of it, later marking their "triumphant return" to the Persian Room in October 1946. Alternating with them on opening night was the Emil Coleman Orchestra, whose performance was broadcast over the Blue Network; live radio shows from the room continued intermittently until the late 1950s.

The Persian Room underwent a number of redecorations over the years, most significantly in 1950 and 1973. The view at right was made two days before it opened. The whiskey bottle and cocktail glasses on the table in the foreground were no doubt carefully arranged to make sure the message was clear: Prohibition was over!

SPANISH DANCING IN A PERSIAN SETTING

The De Marcos—Renée and Antonio—are well known to New Yorkers by their delightful entertaining in the Persian Room of The Plaza, where the Lillian Gaertner Palmedo murals provide a gay and colorful background. Now "In Caliente" has been released from Hollywood, with their dancing a feature of the swift and spicy Mexican picture. Their recent film venture has inspired several of the new dances that they do each evening at The Plaza

THE DE MARCOS
AMERICA'S FOREMOST DANCERS

EMIL COLEMAN
AND HIS RENOWNED DANCE ORCHESTRA

appearing at Dinner and Supper and on Sunday at Dinner and at the Sunday Cocktail Dansant

•

COCKTAIL HOUR DAILY
GEORGE STERNEY
and his Plaza orchestra

The Persian Room at the Plaza

The Persian Room Murals

*A*t left, Lillian Gaertner Palmedo, the artist who painted the Persian Room murals, touches up her work just before the opening, in a photograph no doubt staged for publicity purposes. Given Palmedo's costume and shoes, it seems unlikely that there is any paint on her brush at all.

A minor artist of the thirties, Palmedo is best remembered for the five murals she made for the nightclub, which depicted the pleasures of dancing, hunting, eating, and drinking, Persian-style. Featured conspicuously in advertisements, the murals were forever identified with the room, much in the way that zebra skin was associated with El Morocco; they also launched a brief vogue for all things Persian across the country, when turbans and a color known as Persian blue became fashionable for a time. In 1940, the murals were slightly repainted to harmonize with a new color scheme, then removed altogether when the room was redecorated by Henry Dreyfuss in 1950. Their current whereabouts are unknown.

Below, they are prominently featured on the cover of a 1937 menu.

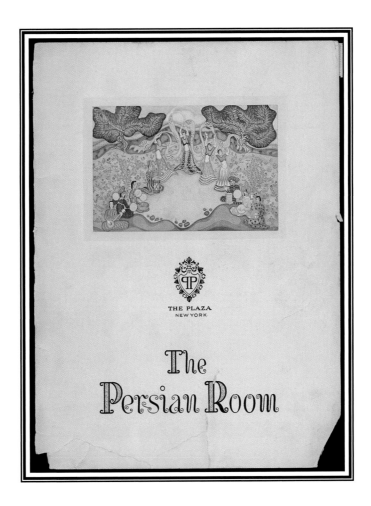

Persian Room Menu, October 14, 1937

*A*lthough some dishes—anchovy canapés, roast partridge, vegetable marrow, cherries jubilee—have gone out of style, such standards as fresh caviar and baby lamb also appear on this fall Persian Room menu.

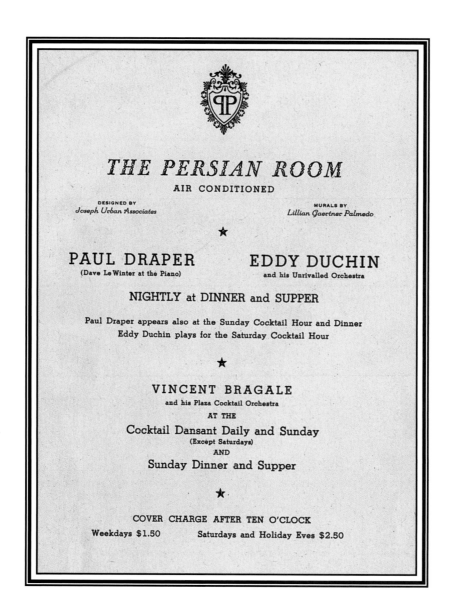

CHAMPAGNE COCKTAIL (Imported) 1 00

DINNER

SEA FOOD

Blue Points 45   Cape Cods or Cotuits 50   Oyster or Clam Relish Lattard 75
Cherry Stone Clams 50   Little Neck Clams 45   Cocktail Sauce 10
Sea Food Cocktail Plaza 1 00   Lobster Cocktail 1 25   Crab Flake Cocktail 75
Shrimp Cocktail 75   Clam Juice or Tomato Juice Cocktail 35

HORS D'OEUVRE

Orange, Grapefruit, Melon or Fruit Supreme 65   Nova Scotia Smoked Salmon 1 00
Plaza Appetizer 1 25   Feuille Suedoise 60   Sturgeon 1 00   Tomato Modern 60
Hors d'Oeuvre Variés   Bismarck Herring 50   Celery 35   Stuffed Celery 50
Maquereau au Vin Blanc 50   Salami 50   Delice Favorite 75   Filet of Herring 50
Fresh Caviar 2 50   Anchovy Canapé 60   Antipasto 50   Westphalian Ham 1 25

SOUPS

St. Germain 40   Julienne aux Pluches 50   Chicken Okra 55   Tomato 40
Cream of Tomatoes with Rice 50   Chicken Broth, Plaza 50
Green Turtle au Madère 80   Boula Gratiné 50

FISH

Boiled Codfish, Sauce Ravigote 90   English Sole, Adrienne 1 50
Frogs' Legs Rissolées Lilloise 1 50   Paupiette of Kingfish, Plaza 1 25
Aiguillette of Mackerel, Marquise 90   Boneless Green Smelts, Florida 1 25
Brook Trout à la Rivièra 1 25   Supreme of Flounder, Waleska 1 00
Sea Bass, Bonne-Femme 1 25   Scallops, Poulette 1 50
Lobster, Excelsior (½) 1 50   Pompano à la Tailer 1 50
Whitebait and Oystercrabs Newburg with Rice Cakes 1 25

ENTREES

Supreme of Chicken Eugénie with New Peas 1 75
Steak Minute, Sauce Bercy, Garnished Niçoise 2 10
Braised Loin of Milk Veal Bourgeoise with Ravioli 1 25
Glazed Ham à la Porte Maillot 1 25   Mushroom Patty, Newburg 1 00
Aiguillette of Duckling Santa Clara, Artichoke Princesse 2 25
Grilled Kernel of Sweetbread, St. Germain 1 50
Mignonette of Spring Lamb, Prince Orloff 1 50

To Order
Smothered Chicken, Marengo (½) 2 00   Royal Squab à la Windsor 2 00
Half Squab-Turkey, Baltimore   Planked American Steak (for 2) 3 95
Filet of Guinea Hen Mikado 2 00   Terrapin à la Maryland 3 00
Partridge en Casserole Grand'mère   Tournedo, President 2 35

ROASTS

Ready—Roast Beef 1 25   Roast Turkey 1 75   Baby Lamb 1 50
To Order—Broiler 3 00 (½) 1 50   Squab-Chicken 2 00
Guinea Hen 3 50   Partridge 3 00

FRESH VEGETABLES

Brussels Sprouts 50   Carrots Vichy 50   Corn Sauté 60   Broccoli or Cauliflower 70
New Peas, String Beans or Lima Beans 60   Parsnips Poulette 60   Succotash 65
Braised Lettuce or Celery 60   Vegetable Marrow 60   Okra à la Créole 75
White Squash 50   Creamed Spinach 60   Stewed Tomatoes 50   Oyster Plant 50
Small Onions in Cream 60   Fried Egg Plant 50   Mashed Yellow Turnips 50
Potatoes—Biron 45   Boiled New 30   Anna 50   Sweet, Plaza or Dixie 50

SALADS

Chatelaine 60   Endive 60   Lettuce, Tomato and Asparagus Tips 60   Jeannette 60
Shrimp or Crab Flake 1 25   Chicken 1 50   Lobster 1 75   Roast Beef Lattard 1 35
Fruit Salad 60   Escarole, Lettuce, Romaine, Mixed Green or Tomato 45

DESSERTS

Apple Charlotte, Hard Sauce 40   Banana Custard Pudding 35
Cherries Jubilée 65   Coffee Bavaroise 40
Pumpkin Pie 35   Fresh Fruit Tart 40   Rice Pudding 35   French Pastry (1) 25
Stewed Fresh Fruit—Plums 50   Pears or Rhubarb 45
Ice Creams—Vanilla, Chocolate, Coffee, Pistachio or Caramel 45   Lalla Rookh 60
Kummel Sherbet 60   Coupe Petit Duc 60   Bombe Rêve de Bébé 60

Cheese—Camembert, Edam, Port du Salut or Bel Paese 45   Imported Swiss 40
Roquefort or Gorgonzola 50   Liederkranz 45   Stilton 60   English Cheddar 50

Fruits—Cantaloupe 50   Spanish or Honey Dew Melon 60   Grapes 50
Sliced Figs 60   Cream 10   Orange, Apple or Bartlett Pear 20

Thursday, October 14, 1937

Conrad Hilton Buys The Plaza

Thirty-six years of continuous original ownership came to an end when The Plaza was sold in 1943 to Conrad Hilton, "the King of Innkeepers," in partnership with the Atlas Corporation, a holding company. Hilton was not yet a builder but, rather, an acquirer of hotels, and he had amassed a fleet of hostelries across the country by buying them at cut-rate post-Depression prices; The Plaza (admittedly not in the best repair at the time) was had for the bargain sum of $7.5 million. Though permanent guests and the old guard braced themselves for a lowering of standards, their fears proved groundless. "I buy tradition and make the most of it," Hilton announced, although he did implement a number of subtle (and not so subtle) alterations that would forever change the place.

These changes were a result of "digging for gold," a Hilton credo for finding ways to maximize profitability in his properties, with prime gold digging usually concentrated in the lobby areas. Thus, Hilton's first action at The Plaza was to remove the brokerage firm of E. F. Hutton from its ground-floor parkside office (monthly rental: $416); in its place, he installed the Oak Bar, immediately one of the hotel's most popular—and lucrative—spaces. Similarly, a basement storage area that once housed the Grill Room was transformed into the Rendezvous supper club, mezzanine writing rooms overlooking the lobby were sealed off and remade into rooms for private functions, and vitrines—glass showcases rented out for product display—were installed for the first time throughout the lobby area. More controversially, the leaded-glass dome over the Palm Court was removed and replaced with a flat baroque ceiling to allow for central air conditioning and even more space for private functions above it.

Hilton retained control of the hotel until 1953. Above, a hotel brochure circa 1950, and at left, the hotelier with singer Hildegarde. Opposite, Hilton proudly poses in front of the Fifth Avenue entrance of his peerless trophy.

Hiltonitems

ACROSS THE NATION

A Magazine for Hilton Employees Everywhere • December, 1946

The Incomparable Hildegarde

The performer most associated with the Persian Room (and record holder for the most performances there—over one hundred weeks) first rose to prominence as a café singer during World War II. Born Hildegarde Loretta Sell, she was simply known by her first name ("the Incomparable" moniker was added later by an overzealous press agent) and began her career as a pianist. Her renown grew after she cut her teeth performing in Europe, and by the time she returned to Manhattan at the start of the war, she had acquired a signature song—"Darling, Je Vous Aime Beaucoup"—as well as several trademark accessories: elbow-length gloves, worn while playing the piano, and an endless supply of lace handkerchiefs (the tent card below right acknowledges her hankies with its own tiny version).

Although she performed in many other city nightclubs, Hildegarde established a cult following at The Plaza, and, at the height of her fame in the forties, she also hosted her own radio show and held endorsement contracts for perfume, nail polish, hosiery, and wallpaper. In addition, she made a notable contribution to the war effort by selling hundreds of war bonds in return for performing a song. Indeed, her rendition of "The Last Time I Saw Paris" epitomizes for a certain generation the heightened emotions of the war years. She made her last appearance in the Persian Room in January 1975, and no doubt she would be performing there today had the room not closed that same year.

Opposite, pictured on the cover of a magazine for Hilton employees, the singer introduces actress Mary Martin to a Persian Room audience; below left, a newspaper advertisement circa 1950.

THE
Persian Room
PRESENTS

*the triumphant return of
the incomparable*

Hildegarde

MARTIN FREED *conductor-pianist*

Ted
Straeter
His Songs, Piano
and Orchestra

MARK MONTE'S
CONTINENTALS

THE
PLAZA

PLaza 9-3000

Fifth Avenue
at 59th Street

Hildegarde!

THE PLAZA
Fifth Avenue at 59th Street

Colonel Serge Obolensky

his significant figure in Plaza history might not be very well known today, but in his time, he was a noted man about town. Born a White Russian prince, Obolensky was educated at Oxford and was married briefly to a Romanov, until forced to flee his homeland by the Bolshevik army. After emigrating to the United States, he married again—and well—taking the hand of Alice Astor, daughter of John Jacob Astor. Through this family connection, he began his career as a hotelier at the Astor-owned St. Regis. During World War II (when he was in his mid-fifties), he served with distinction as a colonel in the U.S. Army Air Forces, parachuting into Sardinia behind German lines.

After the war, he returned to New York (asking to be addressed as *Colonel* Obolensky, as was the fashion at the time), and in 1946, he was named promotion and public-relations director of The Plaza. Though his tenure was brief—only three years—Obolensky left his mark on the hotel, overseeing the Hilton remodeling of the lobbies, the Palm Court, and the Terrace Room. In addition, he created the Rendez-vous restaurant, a Russian-themed boîte in the basement space that once housed the Grill, and initiated celebrity suites in the hotel proper, luxury apartments designed and named for luminaries of that era—designer Christian Dior, author Somerset Maugham, interior decorator Lady Mendl, and photographer Cecil Beaton. More significantly, Obolensky orchestrated a fortieth anniversary party for The Plaza, which resulted in the hotel being called "legendary" for the first time and which set the stage for it being given landmark status twenty-two years later. (Above right, the program for this party.)

Opposite, he is pictured after one of Hildegarde's openings in the Persian Room with the singer and Joseph Binns, then general manager of the hotel. And at left, dancing with Cary Grant's wife, the heiress Barbara Hutton, on Navy Night in the Ballroom.

DINNER
celebrating the
Fortieth Anniversary of
·The Plaza·

Friday, the 3rd of October
Nineteen Hundred and Forty Seven

The Oak Bar

While the Oak Bar has the appearance of being part of Plaza tradition from its inception, it is a relatively new addition, established in 1945. Originally designed as a brokerage office, the space had been converted into an unnamed barroom (an informal adjunct to the much grander watering hole next door) for an eight-year period, beginning in 1912. This incarnation ended with the arrival of Prohibition; the space was then leased to E. F. Hutton for use as a satellite office. When the hotel was acquired by Conrad Hilton, he realized the commercial potential this space's prime location offered, so he summarily moved the brokerage firm to a mezzanine space in the Fifth Avenue lobby and set about reestablishing this area as a bar.

The photograph opposite was made just before the officially named Oak Bar was opened to the public on January 13, 1945. Postwar modernism is reflected in its three-dimensional linoleum and contemporary furnishings done in a red-white-and-black color scheme; a wooden floor and more traditional accessories (that is, brown leather club chairs and banquettes) have taken their place today. The finishing touches that

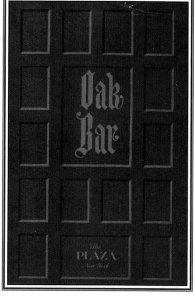

made the room all the more memorable—Everett Shinn's three murals of the hotel—were not yet fully in place when this photograph was taken. Although the painting over the bar can be seen reflected in the mirror, a companion mural on the east wall had yet to be installed.

At left, the mural for the east wall in place, in a picture from a *Life* magazine story. The banquette shown here would later make cinematic history: Cary Grant would be kidnapped from it in the first reel of *North by Northwest*, setting in motion The Plaza's career as a movie star—but that would lie some years ahead. Above, the cover of the room's menu.

The Shinn Murals

A warm, clubby ambience offset by windows overlooking Central Park assured the Oak Bar's popularity from the start, but the three murals by the painter Everett Shinn, commissioned specifically for the room, provided its crowning touch. Shinn began his career in 1897 as a newspaper sketch artist, but he soon turned to fine art, painting realistic urban street scenes. His reputation was made in 1908 after a group exhibition with eight similarly influenced painters (including John Sloan and William Glackens) at New York's Macbeth Gallery. The Eight, as these artists were known—or, more derogatorily, the Ashcan School—shocked aesthetes with their gritty portrayals of contemporary city life. Although Shinn would later turn to the more refined worlds of society and theater for his subject matter, he would forever be identified as an Ashcan painter.

In 1944, he began the Oak Bar murals, three nostalgic scenes of Plaza environs. On the west wall was a mist-shrouded view of Central Park South around 1908, as seen from the vantage point of Columbus Circle. Over the bar was a moonlit rendering of the modern Pulitzer Fountain. The most famous of the murals, a depiction of the open plaza in front of the hotel and the Vanderbilt mansion, decorated the east wall (shown here at right).

The murals' renown and value grew so over the years that every time the hotel changed hands, separate negotiations were undertaken for their purchase. This rather complex arrangement finally came to an end in 1988 when Donald Trump bought the property and the murals for one inclusive sum. Finally, Shinn's art and the hotel that housed it had become inseparable.

The George M. Cohan Corner

A hyphenate long before the word was coined, Broadway's George M. Cohan was a consummate showman, boasting a résumé that included credits as composer, playwright, actor, producer, and theater owner; among his many accomplishments was that of being the only person ever awarded the Congressional Medal of Honor for a song, the rousing World War I anthem "Over There."

By the mid-1930s, it became Cohan's habit to take pretheater cocktails in the Oak Room, and his preferred table was the booth in its northwest corner, which afforded a fine view of all comings and goings. It soon became known as his headquarters, where he was courted by both friends and would-be friends, many of whom were looking for work. After his death in 1942, a number of memorials were proposed in his honor, including a statue to be erected somewhere in the city. The Lambs, a theatrical club, petitioned The Plaza to affix a bronze plaque above the Oak Room booth that he loved so much, and after approval by the Hilton organization, it was put in place on April 24, 1946. The dedication, captured at right, shows Cohan's pals, actors William Gaxton and Victor Moore, along with Raymond Peck, Shepherd of the Lambs, and Plaza owner Conrad Hilton. The plaque remains there to this day, and the Cohan Corner, as it is now known, is still considered the Oak Room's best table.

The municipal statue of Cohan took a lot longer to arrive; it was finally erected in 1959 in Duffy Square on Broadway between Forty-sixth and Forty-seventh streets—a site that, coincidentally, was one of the proposed locales for the Sherman Monument, which instead came to rest in Grand Army Plaza.

Below, Cohan's portrait, taken in the late 1930s by photographer Carl Van Vechten.

The Cecil Beaton Suite

*A*s part of The Plaza's rebirth as a Hilton hotel property, four celebrity suites were created, apartments named for (and, in some cases, designed by) luminaries of the time. The first to be recruited was British photographer Cecil Beaton, an old chum of Serge Obolensky, the mastermind behind the celebrity suites. As part of the agreement, Beaton was allowed to lease the apartment at half price whenever he visited New York.

A large suite, 249–251, was chosen and the redecoration completed in just two weeks at the end of 1945. Furnishing it had been simple enough, for Beaton selected much of the decor from a stock of old hotel furniture that had been banished to a subbasement storage room. The result was eclectic, to say the least: A bust of Racine rested beneath a modern lithograph, while rococo gilt-framed mirrors played off of turn-of-the-century moldings. Beaton remarked, "If you have one good thing in your room, it acts as ballast for the rest," and in this case, the one good thing was a centrally placed coffee table, not rescued from subbasement storage but, instead, purchased specifically for the suite. The resulting stage-set feel (at right) reflected Beaton's latest enthusiasm, set design (among his projects at the time was the staging of the ballet *Moths* and the play *Lady Windermere's Fan*).

Beaton used the suite as his New York base until the early 1950s, when Serge Obolensky decamped from The Plaza for a position at the Sherry-Netherland. Beaton soon followed, and later designed a suite in that hotel that also bore his name.

Greta Garbo in the Cecil Beaton Suite

*I*n February 1946, British designer/photographer Cecil Beaton checked into The Plaza for an extended visit. Not long after he was settled into the suite that he had decorated and which was named in his honor, he was reintroduced to actress Greta Garbo at a cocktail party. The pair had met briefly years before, but this time, something clicked and a friendship began. Beaton, like the rest of the world, was fascinated by the enigmatic star. Five years before, at the height of her fame, Garbo had stopped making movies, and what she would do next was an ongoing topic of public discussion (the answer—nothing—would no doubt have disappointed everyone).

As the friendship developed, Garbo visited Beaton several times at The Plaza, and one day, the subject of her soon-to-expire passport came up. She needed a picture made for the document, and she coyly hinted that she might choose Beaton for the job. He leapt at the chance. The following day, he had the hotel send up a screen to use as a backdrop and pinned a sign on his door: PASSPORT PHOTOS TAKEN HERE.

The star arrived in a buoyant mood, and a few official-looking portraits were taken. Then Beaton suggested some informal shots, and Garbo, to his surprise, agreed. This series of pictures (the "passport photos," as they were archly referred to) was taken by the east window of Room 249 and given the full glamour treatment; Beaton later said that they "crowned my photographic career." Garbo was upset when he sold fourteen of the pictures to *Vogue,* but she maintained an on-again, off-again friendship with Beaton for the rest of her life. Revisionist biographers claim that the pair conducted a four-month-long love affair in Beaton's suite, but this seems unlikely, given what is known of their personal lives. There is no doubt that Beaton was in love, however, as this luminous portrait demonstrates.

At right, the couple on a Manhattan street in 1951, with Garbo assuming a more characteristic pose.

The Duke and Duchess of Windsor Celebrate an Anniversary

*A*lthough more closely associated with the Waldorf-Astoria, where they maintained a residence that still bears their name, the Duke and Duchess of Windsor, one of the most fabled couples of the century, patronized The Plaza frequently after the war. They made a notable public appearance in the hotel's Ballroom on December 11, 1946.

The occasion was the December Ball, a benefit for disabled veterans, and what made it auspicious was that it fell on the tenth anniversary of the duke's abdication of the throne of England in favor of the woman he loved. Though the significance of the abdication had been somewhat diminished following the turmoil of a world war, it still held the public's imagination, and the press came out in record numbers to record the anniversary (at right).

The Windsors appear in a festive mood in the photograph, even if the reality of their future existence was becoming all too plain: They would never be allowed to return to England, and the years ahead would be spent in aimless wanderings among the playgrounds of international society. Still, they presented a united front and carried on in style. As always, they are immaculately turned out here: the duchess in a draped emerald gown, the duke the model of Savile Row chic.

The Rendez-vous

$\mathcal{F}$ollowing the enactment of Prohibition, the subterranean space on the Fifty-ninth Street side that originally housed the Grill Room had been used as a storage area. Conrad Hilton's acquisition of the hotel immediately brought an end to that. Following his dictum of "making the space pay," Hilton asked his resident tastemaker, Serge Obolensky, to remake the room into a restaurant. The result, the Rendez-vous, a nostalgic interpretation of old Russia, was part of the wave of czarist-themed supper clubs that sprouted around Manhattan after the war.

Opened with much fanfare on October 30, 1947, as part of The Plaza's fortieth anniversary celebration, the Rendez-vous was an apricot-and-gold hideaway where two alternating bands—gypsy violinists and a modern orchestra—set the mood. Drama was provided by the house signature dish, shashlik Caucasian, presented at the table on flaming skewers and accompanied by a dimming of the room's lights for full effect.

Obolensky had a following among a certain high-profile crowd, and soon the Rendez-vous counted actress Gertrude Lawrence and the Duke and Duchess of Windsor among its regulars. Its air of chic was maintained on a day-to-day basis, however, by its charismatic maître d', Gigi Molinari. Suave and colorful, Gigi had some very modern ideas about running a nightclub, among which was having an attractive staff, who were dispatched to tanning emporiums in order to acquire year-round suntans. An oft-told anecdote concerns the supper club's opening night, when flaming shashlik Caucasian was about to be served for the first time. The room lights dimmed. In the kitchen, two bronzed waiters eyed their flaming cargo dubiously and turned to Gigi. "Smile, you bastards!" he replied before propelling them onto the floor.

At left, a cover of the room's menu; below, the irrepressible Gigi. Opposite, the restaurant, uncharacteristically deserted, showing the dance floor and bandstand.

Marlene Dietrich in Residence

*I*n the spring of 1948, film legend Marlene Dietrich took up residence at The Plaza for an extended stay. The actress was looking forward to a rest; she had spent most of the war years entertaining Allied troops (winning the Medal of Honor for her efforts) and had just wrapped her first postwar picture, *A Foreign Affair*. There was a new man in her life (whose identity remains a mystery to this day) and it was he who sold her on The Plaza, and, in particular, Suite 317–325. Named after its designer, the noted interior decorator Lady Mendl, the four-room apartment came equipped with mirrored walls, an ornate red antique French clock, and bedroom murals of frolicking nymphs hand-painted by the artist Marcel Vertès. (Below, the parlor of the suite.)

Dietrich immediately banished the clock ("Too much gingerbread," said she) and turned her attention to a more immediate matter: the birth of her first grandchild, who was due in several months. Part of the preparations for the blessed event included the construction of an elaborate wicker bassinet, which Dietrich herself helped to assemble on card tables set up in the parlor of the suite. After the birth, *Life* magazine photographed her by the window of Room 323 and put this picture on its cover, above the headline GRANDMOTHER DIETRICH (opposite), an epithet that later evolved into the title "World's Most Glamorous Grandmother." Although she secretly despised the sobriquet, Dietrich had no choice but to embrace it publicly.

She left The Plaza in June 1949 to meet with Christian Dior in Paris for costume fittings in preparation for her next picture, Alfred Hitchcock's *Stage Fright*. Hitchcock, too, has a history at The Plaza, but he would make his appearance several years later at the filming of *North by Northwest*.

The Christian Dior Suite

While most of Serge Obolensky's celebrity suites in The Plaza honored well-established luminaries, the last to be dedicated was named for a relative newcomer to the celebrity firmament, fashion designer Christian Dior. The couturier burst onto the scene in 1947 with the introduction of his 'New Look,' a collection of luxurious, voluminous dresses that were a reaction to wartime fabric shortages. Immediately embraced by the fashion press as the man of the hour, Dior was a harbinger of a new trend in the culture, the instant celebrity; indeed, by 1949, the Gallup poll would rank him as one of the five most famous people in the world.

His eponymous suite, 223–225, was put together by a transatlantic team of designers based in Paris and New York. They made miniature models of their plans for his approval, and after it was granted, the suite was unveiled to the press on April 21, 1949. The bedroom (below) was done in shades of pale blue and tobacco brown; the parlor (opposite) incorporated beige panels of toile de Jouy on the walls, and an olive green carpet in the latest wall-to-wall style covered the floor. In keeping with an earlier Plaza tradition, no pictures were hung on the walls.

Dior occupied the suite infrequently, and it proved a short-lived experiment. A future tenant, with some very pronounced design ideas of his own, was waiting in the wings. (The following spread shows the same rooms, drastically reinterpreted.)

The Frank Lloyd Wright Suite

*E*arly in 1953, architect Frank Lloyd Wright arrived in New York to oversee construction of the Guggenheim Museum (named after an earlier Plaza resident, art collector Solomon Guggenheim). For the next six years, Wright's Manhattan base would be Suite 223–225 (the former Christian Dior Suite), which he had chosen after a thorough inspection of the house. His choice of The Plaza itself was more automatic: He had been stopping there for years, and he greatly admired Henry Hardenbergh's design. "He built a skyscraper," Wright remarked, "but not the monstrous thing a skyscraper was to become later. He still managed to keep it with a human sense. . . . It's genuine. I like it almost as much as if I'd built it myself"—no small compliment from the usually acerbic critic.

The Christian Dioresque trappings were summarily removed and replaced with objects that reflected the tastes of the new tenant: a piano, drafting table, custom-designed tables and chairs, walls lined with gold Japanese paper, and windows framed by red velvet curtains and topped by circular mirrors that concealed indirect lighting fixtures (the suite's original chandelier was retained). The parlor of Suite 223–225 (at right) was used as a combination office and reception room, while the bedroom (below) was reserved for private use, becoming the domain of Wright's wife. Over time, the suite became known as "Taliesin East," a wry reference to the design schools Wright had founded both in Wisconsin (known simply as Taliesin) and in Arizona (Taliesin West).

After the architect's death in 1959, the furnishings were removed and returned to his Wisconsin home. In 1989, Suite 223–225 was renamed in Wright's honor by Donald and Ivana Trump, who furnished it with authorized reproductions from the Frank Lloyd Wright Foundation.

Photograph © 1999 Pedro E. Guerrero

Photograph © 1999 Pedro E. Guerrero

Frank Lloyd Wright Has His Picture Taken

The images at right came to be taken in a rather round-about way. In 1953, Frank Lloyd Wright was interviewed by Hugh Downs on the *Today* show and gave a spirited talk, punctuated with hand gestures, describing the differences between conventional architecture and "organic" architecture, his own invention. A transcript of the interview was made, then incorporated later into Wright's book *The Future of Architecture*. To illustrate these remarks, the architect reenacted his hand gestures in this series of portraits, shot in the parlor of Suite 223–225 by Pedro Guerrero, Wright's personal photographer for the last twenty years of his life.

The first six photos depict conventional architecture's post-and-beam construction. Wright appears to disapprove, and in views seven through ten, he interlocks his fingers to demonstrate the superiority of organic architecture. In the last two shots, he describes his design concept for the Unitarian Meeting House as "reverent, without recourse to the steeple."

Photographs © 1999 Pedro E. Guerrero

Frank Lloyd Wright ... On Record

*W*henever Frank Lloyd Wright was in residence in Suite 223-225, there was a flurry of activity, and 1956 proved to be a particularly busy year. Among other accomplishments, ground was broken for the Guggenheim Museum, his firm completed fourteen building projects, and Wright himself published *The Story of the Tower,* an account of the construction of the Price Tower in Bartlesville, Oklahoma. Among the many visitors to the suite during this period were newlyweds Marilyn Monroe and Arthur Miller, who came to discuss plans for a summer home. Although this project was never realized, Wright did allow afterward that "Miss Monroe's architecture is extremely good architecture."

In the spring of 1956, shortly before his 89th birthday, he made a recording in the suite. This came about through the efforts of Ben Raeburn, Wright's editor at Horizon Press, his publisher. It was Raeburn who suggested that Wright pose for the photographs on the preceding pages, and Raeburn who arranged this session with Caedmon Records, a label for spoken-word recordings established in 1952. Dylan Thomas, T.S. Eliot, James Joyce, Ernest Hemingway, and William Faulkner were among the illustrious figures that the company recorded.

Along with Raeburn, Marianne Mantell and Barbara Holdridge of Caedmon were present at the recording of what came to be titled "Frank Lloyd Wright . . .On Record." In fact, the moderators had very little to do, as Wright extemporized for nearly two hours with few pauses. Covering a wide range of topics, he began with the pronouncement that all the arts were "minor" compared to the "mother art, architecture," and concluded that "the future of architecture is the future of the human race."

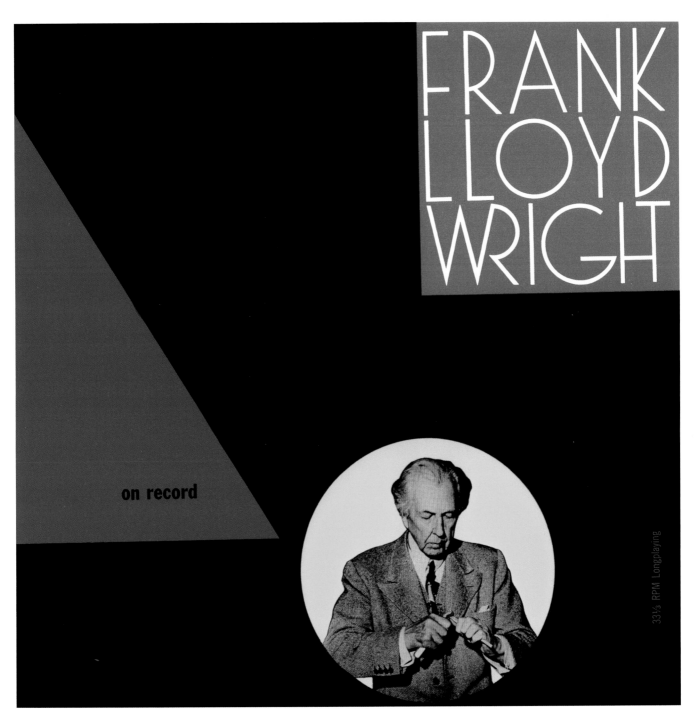

Photograph © 1999 Pedro E. Guerrero

Henry Dreyfuss Transforms the Persian Room

*J*oseph Urban's original Art Moderne style for the Persian Room had been modified several times after its 1934 opening, and as part of Conrad Hilton's general renovation of The Plaza, it was decided to completely modernize it in 1950. Chosen for this project was the noted industrial designer Henry Dreyfuss, whose firm was responsible for many icons of modern design, including the Honeywell round thermostat, the Princess and Trimline telephones, and the Polaroid Land camera. More significantly, Dreyfuss was also responsible for the luxe interiors of the 20th Century Limited supertrain as well as several ocean liner interiors. (The fact that he had been a longtime Plaza regular since the 1930s was also in his favor.)

After a thorough study of Persian motifs, a blue-and-green color scheme was decided upon. Then Dreyfuss stripped the room to its basics, installing two large screens with a white-and-gold diamond pattern as its centerpiece (below), upon which bronze figures depicting Persian hunters were mounted. A raised terrace was constructed around its perimeter, and the finishing touch consisted of metallic mesh curtains, custom-made by Dorothy Liebes. Dreyfuss also designed the china and the menu (at left), which reworked the diamond pattern. The room reopened on September 28, 1950, after $200,000 had been spent on its renovation, and would undergo its next, and final, renovation in 1973.

In the Persian Room

*O*ver its forty-one-year run, the Persian Room showcased a wide variety of talent. In addition to the performers illustrated here, the formidable list also included Eddy Duchin, Kitty Carlisle, the Mills Brothers, Bob Fosse, Jane Powell, Victor Borge, Marge and Gower Champion, Lillian Roth, Eddie Fisher, Henny Youngman, Abbe Lane and Xavier Cugat, the McGuire Sisters, the Lettermen, Connie Stevens, Dinah Shore, Leslie Gore, Shirley Bassey, Vic Damone, Florence Henderson, Doc Severinsen, Lainie Kazan, Dusty Springfield, and Liza Minnelli.

In addition to television and radio broadcasts, a number of recordings were made in the room, shown on the following pages.

Opposite, clockwise from top left: Bob Hope amusing friends onstage, Liberace with Ted Straeter (the room's bandleader), a tent card from the fall of 1971, and Dorothy Kilgallen at a charity auction. This page, tent cards from the 1950s.

This page, newspaper ads for songbirds Ethel Merman and Eartha Kitt (who also made a recording in the room). Opposite, record jacket art from recordings made in the 1950s and 1960s.

You are invited to attend a war.

Miss Ethel Merman will launch an attack on the Persian Room and conquer it from November 6 to November 26. Her secret weapon is nobody's business. Her larynx is something else entirely, having been minted somewhere west of Jericho. Her militia, Emil Coleman's Orchestra and Mark Monte's Continentals, will skirmish now and then, to the latest sennets and alarums. For reservations, please call PLaza 9-3000. And for a lovely evening, the Persian Room at THE PLAZA
HOTEL CORPORATION OF AMERICA

Beware of the kitten!

She purrs in the Persian Room and women watch their men go mad! Eartha Kitt, like fire, is a priceless gift of the gods, but a dangerous plaything. Barely under control, she warms the heart with songs and extraordinary advice. See her, if you dare, from April 10 through May 7. To help you work off steam, Emil Coleman's Orchestra and Mark Monte's Continentals will play dance music. For reservations, PLaza 9-3000. For a lovely evening, the Persian Room at The Plaza. HOTEL CORPORATION OF AMERICA

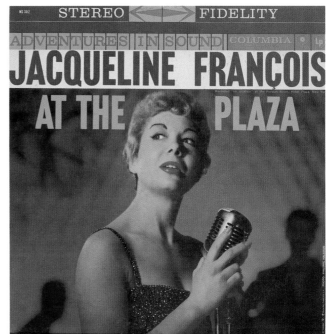

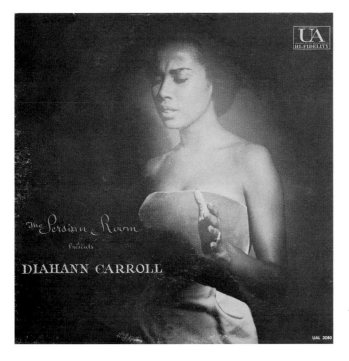

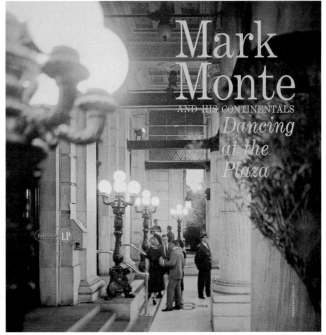

Miss Kay Thompson

*M*any writers have used The Plaza as a setting in their fiction, but few are as closely identified with the place as Kay Thompson, creator of the infamous *Eloise*. Her wry tale about a mischievous six-year-old hotel guest has sold in the millions and become part of Plaza lore, yet *Eloise* was but one of Thompson's many accomplishments.

She began her career as a singer with Fred Waring's band, but she discovered that her talents lay in an emerging field of the music industry, vocal arranging. Signed by the Freed unit at MGM in the 1940s, she is credited with introducing jazz styling into the vocal arrangements of such stars as Judy Garland and Lena Horne during the golden age of Hollywood musicals. (Horne later called her "the best vocal coach in the world.") When her MGM contract expired, she decided to experiment with a new kind of nightclub act, an elab-

orately choreographed program in which she shared the bill with a vocal quartet, the Williams Brothers. Pictured opposite in an ebullient publicity still, the act was a hit and toured for several years. (Trivia buffs might recognize the brother behind Thompson's left shoulder as Andy Williams, before he embarked on a solo career.) Included in their tour were several engagements in the Persian Room; above, an advertisement for an appearance in October 1952; at left, the group performing.

The act eventually broke up, and Thompson wrote *Eloise,* for which she is probably best remembered. Not resting on her laurels, she later appeared in several films, most notably as the Diana Vreeland–like fashion editor in *Funny Face.*

ELOISE sleeps in comfort this summer.

DON'T DISTURB Love

She has an air-conditioned room at THE PLAZA.

ELOISE LIMITED

PLAZA 9-3000

THE PLAZA • FIFTH AVENUE AT FIFTY NINTH STREET
NEW YORK 19, N. Y.

THOMPSON
sident

HERE'S THE THING OF it

DON'T DISTURB Love

POST CARD

I'M ABSOLUTELY THINKING OF YOU
THANKS A LOT

ME, ELOISE

TO MAIL - Remove String

The Plaza
NEW YORK

Please
DO NOT DISTURB

Eloise

Kay Thompson's Eloise, as it is officially titled, has become something of an institution at The Plaza. Published over forty years ago and still going strong, this story of a capricious six-year-old hotel guest has taken on a mythic quality. The character was born in the late 1940s, when Thompson arrived late for a photo session and said by way of explanation, "I am Eloise. I am six." "Talking Eloise" soon evolved into a bit of shtick with the band in her nightclub act, an in-joke that was gradually introduced to the public onstage. When the illustrator Hilary Knight rendered a drawing of the tiny minx, Thompson sensed a kindred spirit and it was decided to immortalize Eloise in print. Written in Thompson's Plaza suite in 1954 and published by Simon and Schuster the following year, the book has remained in print—save one short hiatus—ever since.

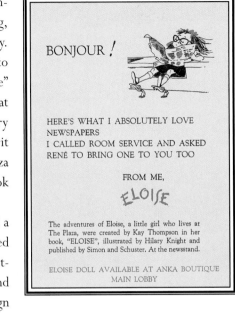

BONJOUR!

HERE'S WHAT I ABSOLUTELY LOVE
NEWSPAPERS
I CALLED ROOM SERVICE AND ASKED
RENÉ TO BRING ONE TO YOU TOO

FROM ME,

ELOISE

The adventures of Eloise, a little girl who lives at The Plaza, were created by Kay Thompson in her book, "ELOISE", illustrated by Hilary Knight and published by Simon and Schuster. At the newsstand.

ELOISE DOLL AVAILABLE AT ANKA BOUTIQUE
MAIN LOBBY

The character quickly became a cottage industry, spawning three sequels and a slew of commercial tie-ins—dolls, recordings, children's clothing—and proved to a marketing bonanza for The Plaza. Opposite, clockwise from top left, is a postcard promoting air conditioned guest rooms, Kay Thompson's business card, and both sides of a Do Not Disturb sign that also doubled as a postcard. This page, flyers advertising newspaper delivery and the Rendez-vous nightclub.

CHEERIO!

NANNIE AND ME ELOISE
   ALWAYS HAVE ROOM SERVICE
THEY ALWAYS GIVE YOU THIS
   NEWSPAPER FOR BREAKFAST
WE ALWAYS ORDER ALL OUR
   OATMEAL AND
   HORS D'OEUVRES
   AND THINGS — AND SAY
CHARGE IT PLEASE
THANK YOU VERY MUCH

ELOISE

"Eloise in Paris" by Kay Thompson, illustrated by Hilary Knight — at the newsstand.

Perhaps the only sour note in the *Eloise* saga came when a *Playhouse 90* television special loosely based on the book aired on Thanksgiving Day, 1956. Despite a stellar cast that included Ethel Barrymore, Louis Jourdan, Monty Woolley, and Evelyn Rudie (center, opposite) in the title role, the show was universally proclaimed a turkey. Eloise has never been dramatized since.

ELOISE AT The Plaza
NEW YORK, N.Y. 10019

Patricia Kennedy Weds Peter Lawford

eddings have long been a Plaza tradition, and one of the more notable nuptials was celebrated in the hotel on April 24, 1954, the day Patricia Kennedy, daughter of Joseph and Rose Kennedy, married British film star Peter Lawford. The ceremony itself was performed at the Roman Catholic church of St. Thomas More on Eighty-ninth Street, followed by a lavish reception in The Plaza's Ballroom.

The Kennedy clan had not yet made itself known as an American political dynasty, so the attendance by the bride's brothers Jack, Bobby, and Teddy (who all served as ushers) meant little to the general public. Rather, it was the bridegroom's Hollywood connection—and attendees like Marion Davies and Greer Garson—that drew three thousand onlookers to the church, and later to The Plaza.

At right, the happy couple. Below, the groom (at center) flanked by his new in-laws, Jacqueline, John, and Robert Kennedy. The reception proved enough of a success that the family again chose The Plaza for Jean Kennedy and Stephen Smith's 1956 wedding reception.

Marilyn Monroe and the Broken Shoulder Strap

hile The Plaza's Terrace Room has seen its share of press conferences, few have caused the pandemonium that occurred on the afternoon of February 9, 1956, when Marilyn Monroe arrived to announce her latest film project. Interest in Monroe was high, as this was her first major appearance since leaving Hollywood for New York the year before.

She had come to promote her latest project, a film based on Terence Rattigan's play *The Sleeping Prince* (released as *The Prince and the Showgirl*). Accompanying her was the playwright and her future costar, Laurence Olivier, yet no one paid either man much attention. Marilyn, clad in a snug black velvet dress with thin straps and a matching jacket, was clearly the draw. The press conference proceeded routinely enough to begin with, until the actress removed her jacket, leaned forward—and broke a shoulder strap. After a moment of stunned silence, a blaze of flashbulbs erupted. A safety pin was called for, but even

after a quick repair, the strap broke again, to the accompaniment of even more flashbulbs. "Shall I take off my coat, boys?" Laurence Olivier offered feebly. "Does anybody care?"

The broken strap put Monroe on front pages across the country—times were simpler then—although it was hardly an accident. According to the designer of the star's dress, the strap-breaking incident was prearranged and carefully engineered in advance. "Just wait and see what's going to happen," the actress told a photographer before making her entrance and her unique contribution to Plaza legend.

Jayne Mansfield in the Tricycle Garage

$\mathcal{F}$ollowing the rousing success of *Eloise*, The Plaza realized the value of cultivating the toddler set (and their indulgent parents), and thus the idea of the Tricycle Garage was born. (It came about after general manager Eugene Voit—the father of a six-year-old—discovered firsthand how difficult it was to maneuver a child and tricycle into Central Park and back for some bike riding.) Carved out of a corner of the Fifty-eighth Street loading dock and done up in jolly red-and-white candy stripes, the garage opened in May 1956 and provided bike racks and numbered license plates for a fee of fifteen cents a day or three dollars per month. Plaza guests were allowed to use it gratis and were also loaned tricycles for free. (Bottom, a handout card announcing the service.)

The promotion proved popular enough to inspire a special children's menu (bottom right, featuring Eloise on a three-wheeler), available in all of the restaurants. Among its offerings were Sirloin Suzie-Q, Teeny Weenies, and Mary-Had-a-Little-Lamb Chop, which could be accompanied by a Kiddie Kar Kocktail. The pièce de résistance was the Tricycle Treat, a dessert featuring a tiny bike rider cast in vanilla ice cream, riding on a square of sponge cake in a drift of whipped cream doused with raspberry sauce.

At the time of the garage's unveiling, Hollywood starlet Jayne Mansfield was in the city promoting her latest picture, *The Girl Can't Help It*. An overamplified version of Marilyn Monroe, Mansfield was always game for any kind of publicity, and opposite she poses dutifully with her daughter, Jayne Marie.

LET YOUR CHILD
BE OUR GUEST!

Take your tiny tot for a tricycle trip through Central Park — leaving from our
TRICYCLE GARAGE!

Call Mr. Pisapia,
Assistant Manager.

THE PLAZA
New York

HILARY KNIGHT

Edwardian Room Menu, November 8, 1956

*T*he space offhandedly referred to as The "Plaza Restaurant" was finally given an official name, the Edwardian Room, in 1955. Its staid elegance is reflected in this winter menu.

The Edwardian Dinner

Treat For The Tiny Tots-
Bring your little folks to
The Plaza on their
Three-Wheelers.
Use our Tricycle Garage
for Free Parking.

Any Choice of Listed Courses

$5.00

Tomato or Clam Juice Cocktail   Filet of Herring, Sour Cream and Onions
Fruit Suprême   Antipasto Plaza   Hearts of Artichoke, Vinaigrette
Clam or Shrimp Cocktail   Imported Salami   Pâté Maison
Blue Point Oysters   Cape Cod Oysters

or

Cream of Mushrooms, St. Denis   Consommé Miranda
Split Pea Soup   Jellied Madrilene   Vichyssoise

Filet of English Sole, Mervina, Olivette Potatoes Persillées
Brook Trout Sauté with Mushrooms and Asparagus Tips

Hot House Chicken en Casserole, Chez-Soi (Half)
Milk Veal Chop Sauté au Madère with Mushrooms, Whole Spinach
Breast of Duckling with Black Cherries, Montmorency, Wild Rice
Roast Spring Lamb au Romarin, Parisiènne Potatoes, New Peas à l'Etuvée
ROAST PRIME RIBS OF BEEF AU CRESSON WITH BAKED POTATO (75c. EXTRA)

———

Chiffonade Salad - By Request
Low Calorie Dressing Upon Request

Apple or Pumpkin Pie   Fruit Tart   French Pastry
Fruit Jello, Whipped Cream   Lemon Meringue Pie   Ice Cream or Sherbet
Bread and Butter Pudding   Custard Rice Pudding with or without Raisins
Compote of Fruits   Assorted Cheese

———

Demi-Tasse

Thursday, November 8, 1956

A la Carte

Appetizers

Blue Point Oysters 90   Cape Cod Oysters 95
Little Neck Clams 85   Tomato, Vege-Crest, Clam Juice or V-8 Cocktail 55   Cherrystone Clams 90
Lobster Cocktail 2 85   Crab Flake Cocktail 1 80   Shrimp Cocktail 1 70

Hors d'Oeuvres Variés, Plaza 2 50   Filet of Herring in Sour Cream, Onions 95
Beluga Malossol Caviar 5 70   Fruit Suprême 95
Terrine of Imported Foie Gras 4 25   Prosciutto Ham 2 65   Smoked Sturgeon 2 60
Imported Filet of Tunafish 2 25   Smoked Salmon 1 95   French or Portugaise Sardines 1 70
Plaza Antipasto 1 15   Imported Mackerel in White Wine, Portion 1 85; Can 3 70   Imported Salami 1 95

Soups

Cream of Mushrooms, St. Denis 70   Consommé Miranda 60
Split Pea Soup 70   Green Turtle Soup 1 20   Strained Gumbo 70   Chicken Okra 70
Chicken Broth with Rice 60   Jellied Madrilene 60   Cold Vichyssoise 60

Fish

Broiled Red Snapper, Maître d'Hôtel, Nest Printanière 2 60
Filet of English Sole, Mervina, Olivette Potatoes Persillées 3 50
Brook Trout Sauté with Mushrooms and Asparagus Tips 3 55
Baked Fresh Salmon with Brunoise of Vegetables, Livournaise 3 20

Entrees

Hot House Chicken en Casserole, Chez-Soi (Half) 3 15
Larded Sirloin of Beef, Forestière, with Cèpes, Broccoli, Potatoes Dauphine 4 90
Milk Veal Chop Sauté au Madère with Mushrooms, Whole Spinach 3 20
Breast of Duckling with Black Cherries, Montmorency, Wild Rice 4 15
Roast Spring Lamb au Romarin, Parisiènne Potatoes, New Peas à la Etuvée 3 65
Broiled Venison Steak, Sauce Poivrade, Brussels Sprouts, Fried Hominy 4 30

Specialties ⁓ Prepared at Your Table

MARYLAND CRABMEAT, MONSEIGNEUR 3.50
SCALLOPINI OF VEAL A LA TREVI 3.75
MEDAILLON OF BEEF AU CHAMBERTIN 5.50
VEAL KIDNEY AU ROMARIN, FLAMBE AU COGNAC 2.95

——————————

Roasts and Grill

Grain Fed Chicken en Casserole (For 2) 6 30   Broiled Chicken (Half) 2 80   Lamb Chop (1) 2 35; (2) 4 35
L. I. Duckling (For 2) 7 40   Pheasant Souvaroff (For 2) 13 00   Royal Squab 3 80   French Lamb Chop 3 55
Sirloin Steak 6 80   Sirloin Steak (For 2) 13 10   Minute Steak 6 30   Filet Mignon 6 80
Vibo Farm Rock Cornish Hen aux Primeurs 4 60   Baby Turkey (Half) (For 2) 6 95

Cold Buffet

Maine Lobster with Cucumber and Tomato Salad, Mayonnaise (Half) 3 55
Smoked Brook Trout, Knob Celery Salad 3 55   Crab Meat Ravigotte 2 65
Assorted Cold Cuts with Turkey and Potato Salad 3 15   Imported Danish Ham, Asparagus Tips 3 30
Roast Beef, String Beans Salad 4 80   Beef Tongue, Beet Salad 2 60   Roast Chicken (Half) 2 80

Vegetables

Artichoke with Drawn Butter 1 00   Imported White Asparagus 2 45   Belgian Endive Meunière 1 00
Creamed Succotash 85   Lima Beans 75   Baked Tomato 70   Braised Celery with Marrow 90
Zucchini 85   Grilled Mushrooms 1 25
Cauliflower, Gratiné 95   Small Carrots 80   String Beans 75   Peas 75
Broccoli Mousseline 1 00   Whole Spinach 70   Brussels Sprouts 75   Spinach in Cream 85
Potatoes: French Fried 55   Baked 60   ·   Parisiènne 60   Purée or Parsley 55

Salads

Salade du Chef 2 10   Avocado with Grapefruit 1 00   Cucumber 75   Mixed Greens 80
Heart of Palm 1 15   Romaine 75   Belgian Endive 1 00   Lettuce and Tomato with Green Pepper 85
Low Calorie Dressing Upon Request

Desserts

Apple or Pumpkin Pie 60   Fruit Tart 60   French Pastry 50
Compote of Fruits 90   Lemon Meringue Pie 60   Caramel Custard, Beau Rivage 50
Custard Rice Pudding with or without Raisins 55   Pot de Crème Vanille, Café ou Chocolat 50

Ices

Special Tricycle Treat .95

Pistachio, Strawberry, Chocolate, Vanilla or Coffee Ice Cream 70   Neapolitan Delight, Sabayon Sauce 1 30
Frozen Roll, Strawberry Sauce 95   Ice Cream Filled Eclair with Butterscotch Sauce 90
Coupe aux Marrons 90   Plaza Parfait 90   Strawberry Sundae 95   Nectar Glacé, Monseigneur 90
Sorbet à l'Orange, Citron, Ananas ou Framboise 70; with Liqueur 95   Peach Melba 90

Cheese

Cheddar 70   Swiss 75   Port du Salut 70   Camembert 70   Blue 75
Swiss Gruyère 70   Brie 80   Cream 70   Gold-N-Rich 70   Liederkranz 70   Bel Paese 75

Fruits

Grapes 80   Orange 45   Grapefruit 70   Bartlett Pear 50   Golden or Delicious Apple 45
Strawberries 1 00; with Cream 1 35   Melon in Season 1 00   Sliced Bananas in Cream 90

Coffee, Tea, Etc.

Coffee 45   Cream Portion 15   Tea, Plain, or with Lemon 40
Demi Tasse 35   Yogurt 55   Milk, Half Pint 30
Café Filtre (For 1 or 2) 1 10   (For 3 or 4) 2 20

Thursday, November 8, 1956   SERVICE CHARGE 30 CENTS

Alfred Hitchcock's *North by Northwest*

Alfred Hitchcock's classic thriller marked the beginning of a watershed era for The Plaza, the launch of its movie career. Although the hotel had made earlier cameo appearances in pictures like *Gentlemen's Agreement* (usually a fleeting background appearance as part of the skyline), *North by Northwest* marked something different: the first time an entire movie company—director, actors, and crew—came together on the site of The Plaza to make a film. This was rather unusual for that period, as Hollywood pictures were made on Hollywood sets for the most part, rarely on location. This equation would reverse itself by the end of the century, however; indeed, location shooting would become so commonplace that The Plaza would appear in thirty-four features and claim the title of New York's most popular film site by the year 2000.

North by Northwest is vintage Hitchcock—a convoluted case of mistaken identity—and shooting commenced in August 1958, with the scenes that opened the movie: Cary Grant being kidnapped from table 2 in the Oak Bar, followed by a later sequence where he eludes his would-be captors and manages a successful escape through the Fifty-ninth Street door (pictured below). A resounding success for Hitchcock both critically and commercially, the picture garnered Oscar nominations for its script, art direction, and editing. Many years later, the American Film Institute would compile a list of the greatest films of the century and rank *North by Northwest* at a very respectable number 40.

Opposite, Cary Grant tears through the lobby followed by actress Jessie Royce Landis, who was a year younger than Grant, but played his mother in the film nevertheless.

Above, Alfred Hitchcock affects nonchalance in the Fifty-ninth Street lobby during shooting.

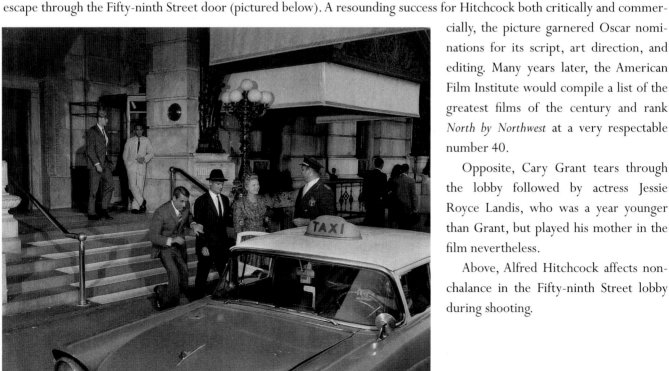

Jazz at The Plaza

*M*odern jazz made a spectacular debut at The Plaza on September 9, 1958, when Columbia Records showcased selected artists at a by-invitation-only affair in the Persian Room. The invitation simply read "Come to a Jazz Party," a marvel of understatement given its stellar cast of performers.

Duke Ellington and his orchestra led off the program with "Jazz Festival Suite," and after a short set, they yielded the stage to the Miles Davis Sextet (which at the time included John Coltrane and Cannonball Adderley); among their offerings was Davis's original composition "Jazz at The Plaza." Ellington returned for the second half of the show, accompanying singer Jimmy Rushing, but before closing with a spirited version of "Take the 'A' Train," a late arrival to the party took the stage: Lady Day herself, Miss Billie Holiday, who sang "Hush Now Don't Explain" and "When Your Lover Has Gone," and brought down the house. Sadly, this proved one of the singer's last appearances in New York City; she had less than a year to live.

Happily, the concert was recorded, although with no immediate thought of commercial distribution. The tapes from this mythic evening lay in Columbia's vaults until 1973, when they were released on two LPs entitled *Jazz at The Plaza* (jacket art below).

At left, photographer Don Hunstein's portraits of Duke Ellington on the bandstand and Billie Holiday and Miles Davis after the show.

Ike and Mamie and Jack and Jackie

*P*oliticians have always been a presence at The Plaza, and every U.S. president since William Taft has made an appearance there. Though some came just for the fun of it—Harry Truman was fond of lunching in the Palm Court with his daughter, Margaret, and Richard Nixon was a regular at Trader Vic's—most politicians showed up to be honored at various fund-raising testimonials.

Among them were two pivotal figures of 1950s American politics, Dwight D. Eisenhower and John F. Kennedy. The Eisenhowers, pictured below with Jacqueline Cochran Odlum and her husband, Floyd, attended a Baroque Room dinner in honor of Mrs. Odlum, the country's leading aviatrix. (Her husband, not incidentally, controlled the Atlas Corporation, which co-owned The Plaza along with Conrad Hilton.)

Senator and Mrs. John F. Kennedy (at right) graced the Ballroom on December 8, 1959, for a fancy dress Wild West Ball benefiting a pet charity, the Kennedy Child Study Center for Retarded Children. The senator's string tie (and hidden gun belt, worn under his jacket) as well as Mrs. Kennedy's demure dance-hall-gal ensemble were in keeping with the western theme of the evening.

The Second British Invasion of America

*I*t all began rather innocently: a hotel booking made several weeks in advance for a small group of Englishmen. None of their names—Lennon, McCartney, Harrison, Starr—meant anything to the staff until a copy of *Life* magazine landed on general manager Alphonse Salomone's desk, opened to a story entitled "Four Screaming Moptops Break Up England. Here Come Those Beatles." Salomone knew that there was no question that the reservations would be honored, but he wasn't naïve, and so, in short order, the police commissioner was notified, extra security was hired from Burns Guards, and six small suites for the British guests were blocked out on the Fifty-eighth Street side of the twelfth floor (intentionally away from the main entrances, with windows that faced inside to the hotel courtyard).

Living up to their press clippings, the Beatles arrived on February 7, 1964, in a burst of fanfare. The crowd at the airport followed them to the hotel, then encamped there for the next five days (below). About the most serious infraction of hotel security occurred when two teenage girls managed to smuggle themselves up to the twelfth floor inside a gift box, but they were summarily escorted out. Hotel personnel found the Beatles to be pleasant and unassuming, and quick to oblige when people made photo requests; at left, Ringo, Paul, and George pose with Christina Krupka, in a photograph taken by her father, Henry, the owner of D'Arlene Studios. Krupka's studio was situated off the Fifth Avenue lobby, and he is responsible for many of the photographs in this book dating from the 1950s and 1960s.

The Beatles' Press Conference

The press unabashedly loved the Beatles, taken by their new, cheeky version of celebrity, and the fact that these irreverent upstarts were ensconced in the posh Plaza only made the story better. The Beatles returned the favor by giving the media something to write about. Over the five days that the Fab Four spent in Manhattan, they appeared on *The Ed Sullivan Show,* gave a press conference, partied at the Playboy Club and the Peppermint Lounge, and performed back-to-back concerts at Carnegie Hall.

The press conference (pictured below) was held on February 10, 1964 in The Plaza's Baroque Room, where the group was presented a pair of gold records for their album *Meet the Beatles* and their single "I Wanna Hold Your Hand." Dr. Joyce Brothers reported the event for the *New York Journal-American,* and at right, Ringo takes her pulse, for reasons now unknown but no doubt amusing at the time. Dr. Brothers had the last laugh, however. The following day, her column, "Why They Go Wild Over the Beatles," summarized their appeal: "The Beatles display a few mannerisms which almost seen a shade on the feminine side, such as the tossing of their long manes of hair. . . . These are exactly the mannerisms which very young female fans appear to go wildest over."

The Two Eloise Portraits

*A*fter the publication of *Eloise,* The Plaza undertook a number of promotions to publicize it. Among these was a portrait painted by the book's illustrator, Hilary Knight, which was hung in the lobby opposite the Palm Court in 1957. It quickly became a favorite of mothers and their daughters, and a much-photographed site.

On Thanksgiving night 1960, following a college dance in the Ballroom, the six-by-four-foot portrait disappeared. Despite nationwide press coverage, it did not turn up. Nor was it immediately replaced, for the book had gone out of print and Eloise's popularity appeared to have crested. It was only after Alphonse Salomone, the hotel's general manager, took Princess Grace of Monaco and her children on a tour of the property that the idea of replacing it was revived. The princess remarked on the portrait's absence, which stuck in Salomone's mind—he himself was a character in the story—and after the book came back into print, it was decided to have the portrait redone. (Opposite, the artist poses beside the second version with an unknown, but obviously fervent, Eloise fan.)

The picture was unveiled on April 17, 1964, as part of the festivities celebrating the opening of the New York World's Fair, and the Beatles, who had recently stayed in the hotel, to much fanfare, sent a congratulatory telegram (below left). The original portrait (bottom right) was never recovered; the second version remains in place opposite the Palm Court—bolted to the wall.

WESTERN UNION TELEGRAM

CLASS OF SERVICE
This is a fast message unless its deferred character is indicated by the proper symbol.

SF-1201 (4-60)

SYMBOLS
DL=Day Letter
NL=Night Letter
LT=International Letter Telegram

W. P. MARSHALL, PRESIDENT

The filing time shown in the date line on domestic telegrams is LOCAL TIME at point of origin. Time of receipt is LOCAL TIME at point of destination

AHB310 AH-NE257
PD NEW YORK NY 14 508P EST   1964 APR 14 PM 5 51
ELOISE, CARE PLAZA HOTEL ROOM 129 ATTN EVE OROWN
   NYK
DEAR ELOISE, WE WISH WE COULD HOLD YOUR HAND. YEAH YEAH YEAH
   THE BEATLES
(44).

Trader Vic's

his legendary restaurant was born in Oakland, California, in 1934. That summer, restaurant owner Victor Bergeron returned from a vacation in Tahiti and introduced native Chinese and Javanese dishes to the menu of his modest establishment, Hinky Dink's. More significantly, he also added sweet, potent rum drinks to the bar offerings, redid the place in faux tropics style, and changed its name to Trader Vic's. The revamping proved enough of a success that it gradually evolved into a chain over the years, with twenty-three outlets at its peak. (Bergeron's other claim to fame—the introduction of the mai tai cocktail stateside—came about after another South Seas sojourn in 1944.)

A prototype of the theme restaurants that would proliferate toward the end of the century, Trader Vic's first debuted in Manhattan at the Savoy-Plaza Hotel in 1958. When that hotel was demolished to make way for the General Motors Building, the restaurant moved across the street to The Plaza's basement, opening in August 1965. In its new home, it replaced what was originally a Turkish bath and later the hotel barbershop with a restaurant whose decor was a kitschy mix of fishnet, thatched ceilings, and South Seas carvings, crowned by the outrigger canoe from the film *Mutiny on the Bounty* mounted in the entry hall. Movers and shakers took to it at once, among them Jacqueline Onassis, Salvador Dalí, Richard Nixon, and the couple pictured below, diva Maria

Callas and fashion designer Oleg Cassini, together for an occasion long ago forgotten.

Trader Vic's closed in 1993 after an impressive twenty-eight-year run. An entire generation would carry fond, if blurry, memories of its signature Fog Cutters, Scorpions, and Tidal Waves. Above, the rather racy cover of its menu.

Mr. Capote Throws a Party

*A*fter six years in the making, *In Cold Blood,* Truman Capote's masterwork, was published in January 1966. It proved to be such a runaway success that it wasn't long before the author began to think about throwing a party—a *big* party— to celebrate. A date was selected, November 28, 1966, and a site, The Plaza's Ballroom. Since it wouldn't do to promote one's own good fortune so blatantly, Capote decided to throw a party in honor of his friend Kay Graham, publisher of the *Washington Post.*

No detail was overlooked in its planning. He chose The Plaza "because it has the only beautiful ballroom left in New York," and the buzz began soon after he engaged the space. It was to be a theme party, with the guests to wear either black or white, as well as masks, which were to be removed at midnight. The guest list was exclusive and eclectic; Capote, after all, had been a player in international society for many years. To assure even more exclusivity, he told his guests whom they could or could not bring as escorts, so that no one would be allowed in without his approval. These four ingredients—a brilliant setting, a select guest list, a strict dress code, and the novelty of wearing masks—proved an irresistible mix. The party was an event long before it happened, and those without invitations begged and cajoled and offered bribes, and, failing all else, they made sure they were out of town so they could explain their absence that night. (Below, the much-coveted invitation.)

Capote rented Suite 437 for the evening, where he had a private dinner with Kay Graham before the party. Opposite, he adjusts his mask in the suite's foyer, surely unaware that what was about to transpire would surpass his wildest dreams.

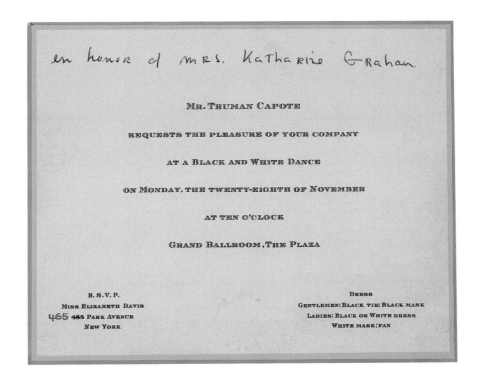

en honor of MRS. KaTharino Grahan

MR. TRUMAN CAPOTE

REQUESTS THE PLEASURE OF YOUR COMPANY

AT A BLACK AND WHITE DANCE

ON MONDAY, THE TWENTY-EIGHTH OF NOVEMBER

AT TEN O'CLOCK

GRAND BALLROOM, THE PLAZA

R. S. V. P.
MISS ELIZABETH DAVIS
465 485 PARK AVENUE
NEW YORK

DRESS
GENTLEMEN: BLACK TIE; BLACK MASK
LADIES: BLACK OR WHITE DRESS
WHITE MASK; FAN

The Black and White Ball

The evening of this fabled party began inauspiciously. It was raining, although this did nothing to dampen the spirits of the 300 onlookers on the street, the 200 press people in the lobby, or the 540 elect whom Capote invited. His guest list read like an international *Who's Who:* Norman Mailer, Rose Kennedy, Steven Sondheim, Henry Fonda, Lillian Hellman, the Maharaja of Jaipur, Lauren Bacall, John Steinbeck, Lynda Bird Johnson, Arthur Miller, Vivien Leigh, Jerome Robbins, Diana Vreeland, James Michener, and Andy Warhol, among others. At right, guest of honor, Kay Graham, and designer Billy Baldwin; opposite, Frank Sinatra and Mia Farrow—arguably the couple of the night, as they were newly wed—linger in the Ballroom foyer.

The Ballroom (below) had been done in red, with not a flower in sight—"The people are the flowers," declared Capote. To the accompaniment of Peter Duchin's orchestra, 450 bottles of Taittinger champagne were served, along with a midnight buffet of chicken hash with sherry, spaghetti Bolognese, and scrambled eggs. The masks came off long before midnight, but other than that minor detail, all of Capote's wishes had been realized.

The party cost Capote sixteen thousand dollars, a modest investment for the millions of dollars' worth of publicity it generated for him. The *New York Times* printed the guest list. CBS aired live coverage. Newspapers across the country offered up editorials debating the meaning of it all. Critic Diana Trilling summed it up neatly, if enigmatically: "a very complicated moment in this country's social history." Magnified by the hyperbolic atmosphere of the 1960s, the Black and White Ball quickly became legendary, and today is a leading candidate for Party of the Century.

Svetlana

orld affairs took center stage at The Plaza on the morning of April 26, 1967, when Svetlana Alliluyeva, the only daughter of Joseph Stalin, held a televised news conference in the Terrace Room. Alliluyeva had just defected to the United States—an unimaginable propaganda coup for the West in its ongoing Cold War with the Soviet Union—and had agreed to meet the press to make a statement, as well as to publicize her forthcoming autobiography. Questions were submitted in writing, in advance, only "because it's a little bit difficult for me sometimes to guess American English," she said. Out of three hundred submissions, thirty-eight were answered in the hour-long conference.

Among other statements, Alliluyeva announced that she had defected "to seek the self-expression that has been denied me for so long in Russia." She also admitted to loving her father but disliking his policies, and then she was asked if she would apply for U.S. citizenship. "I think that before the marriage there should be love," she replied. "So, if I should love this country and this country will love me, then the marriage will be settled. But I cannot say now."

Her comments were well received, and the newsmen applauded at the end of the press conference. Afterward, Alliluyeva spent the rest of the afternoon in her fourteenth-floor Plaza suite, before dropping out of sight to complete work on her memoir. Published in October 1967 by Harper & Row, *Twenty Letters to a Friend* went on to become a bestseller. Alliluyeva eventually became a U.S. citizen and settled in Princeton, New Jersey.

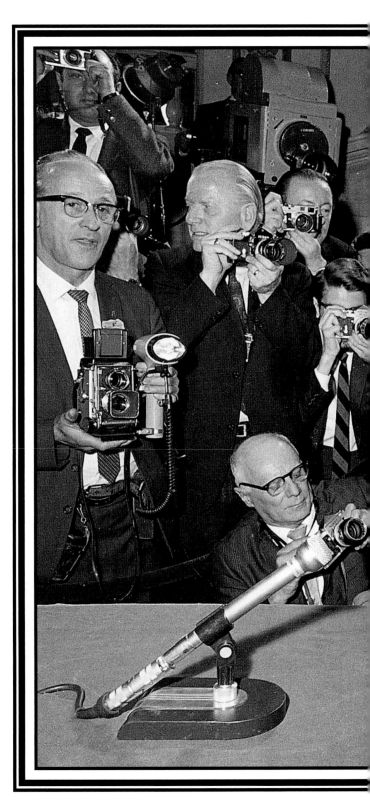

Neil Simon's *Plaza Suite*

*H*aving conquered film and television, The Plaza entered the footlight arena on February 14, 1968, when Neil Simon's *Plaza Suite* opened on Broadway. Simon was then at the peak of his popularity, with four of his shows running simultaneously on the Great White Way and two of them—*The Odd Couple* and *Sweet Charity*—being made into movies. *Plaza Suite* seemed a sure thing, further bolstered by a heavyweight director, Mike Nichols, and stellar cast, Maureen Stapleton and George C. Scott.

The premise of the show was simplicity itself. Performed in three acts, it chronicled three couples' stays in the same Plaza apartment, Suite 719, with Stapleton and Scott playing the various couples. (A fourth act was cut in rehearsals and later reworked into a film, *The Out-of-Towners*.) An immediate hit, the comedy ran for two and a half years on Broadway, countless times on the road, and remains a repertory staple for many regional theaters to this day.

Not surprisingly, it was made into a movie starring Walter Matthau, with Maureen Stapleton, Lee Grant, and Barbara Harris as his respective foils. Although shot in part on location (with Plaza Suite 723 standing in for the fictional 719), the majority of the filming was done on a Hollywood set (seen in the publicity still below), meticulously re-created with props furnished by the hotel. The picture opened at Radio City Music Hall in June 1971, and it proved successful enough to inspire a 1987 remake

for television, starring Carol Burnett. The playwright himself liked the structure of the piece well enough to write two sequels of sorts: *California Suite,* a movie set in the Beverly Hills Hotel, and *London Suite,* a play set in that city's Connaught Hotel.

Above, the *Playbill* for the Broadway show picturing George C. Scott and Maureen Stapleton; opposite, the rather overwrought poster for the film.

Richard Burton and Elizabeth Taylor Meet the Press

𝒯he Terrace Room, Monday, February 5, 1968, 11:30 A.M. Elizabeth Taylor and Richard Burton, the most famous couple in the world at that moment, meet the press to promote their latest film, *Doctor Faustus.* Despite Miss Taylor's chinchilla bonnet and coat, the Burtons had not ventured outdoors for this appearance; they had been in residence on the fourteenth floor for three days, having arrived in true movie star fashion—via motorcade—with four assistants and over sixty pieces of luggage. Preparation for their visit had prompted a flurry of interhotel memos, including instructions to "reserve the best suite available. . . . Arrange to hold our largest safe deposit box. . . . Only address Elizabeth Taylor as 'Mrs. Burton.' . . . Contact Mr. Burton's assistant and diplomatically point out that men's polo neck sweaters and ladies' high fashion silk trousers are not permitted in Plaza restaurants. . . . "

The Terrace Room was built during the enlargement of the hotel in 1921, and it has witnessed many a press conference, among them those of Marlene Dietrich (who admitted to being fifty-three years old) and Woody Allen (who declared his love for his former companion's daughter). In the photos shown here, the curtains behind the Burtons hide doors to the Palm Court, which are sometimes opened to combine the two rooms into one very large multileveled space.

Julie Nixon Weds David Eisenhower

Although her father had been elected president the previous month, First Daughter–elect Julie Nixon did not care to wait until January for a White House wedding. Her engagement to David Dwight Eisenhower II, grandson of another U.S. president, had been announced the year before and the wedding set for December 22, 1968, and that it would be. She wanted a traditional, private wedding: the ceremony at Manhattan's Marble Collegiate Church, conducted by the Reverend Norman Vincent Peale, and the reception in The Plaza's Ballroom.

The bride had been equally vehement about barring the press from the wedding and reception, so a compromise was worked out. After the ceremony, the wedding party would repair to The Plaza's Persian Room, where maroon curtains had been hung as a backdrop for picture taking. Photographs were taken according to plan (at right, the bride and groom kiss) and then the press was dismissed and the wedding party repaired to the Ballroom.

The reception was low-key, with the Ballroom lightly adorned with holly, and seating was equally casual, with no reserved tables. The five hundred guests included the future vice president Spiro Agnew, the president-elect's future cabinet, and various well-connected Republicans, such as Thomas Dewey, the former governor of New York, Clare Boothe Luce, the former U.S. ambassador to Italy, and J. Edgar Hoover, director of the FBI. (The bridegroom's grandparents had been hospitalized and were therefore unable to attend.) Tricia Nixon, sister of the bride and maid of honor, caught the bouquet; Richard Nixon's friend Bebe Rebozo snagged the garter.

Press reports also noted that despite the auspiciousness of the occasion, The Plaza managed to host wedding receptions for six other couples on the same day.

NOW Stages a Protest

Women's liberation arrived at The Plaza on February 12, 1969, the day the National Organization for Women (more commonly known as NOW) staged a sit-in. Their target was the Oak Room, in protest of its men-only policy at lunch, a target that had been shrewdly selected: NOW, founded in 1966, was trying to make a name for itself, and its president, Betty Friedan, very deliberately picked The Plaza for the kind of upscale publicity it would lend to the cause. And since the protest came in the wake of a blizzard, she urged demonstrators to wear fur coats, not only for warmth but also to convey their respectability—and to differentiate NOW from the radical feminists who had recently caused an uproar by burning their brassieres at the Miss America Pageant.

The protest at the Fifth Avenue entrance began on schedule (at right), but Friedan arrived late, clad in a black mink and sunglasses. (The sunglasses were not part of the political agenda; Friedan's husband, upon hearing of the protest, had blackened her eye in an unsuccessful effort to keep her from attending.) Upon her arrival, the group proceeded to the Oak Room, swept past the maître d' and settled at a round table in the center of the room. There they waited—and waited—until four waiters appeared, hoisted the table up, and removed it from the room, leaving the women sitting awkwardly in a circle. A man at a nearby booth offered bread sticks, which were declined. Finally, Friedan announced to the reporters (who outnumbered the protestors), "It looks like we are not going to be served." With that, the group departed.

As anticipated, the protest garnered a lot of press coverage, and the incident proved instrumental in NOW's ascendancy to the front ranks of the American feminist movement. Nor was it in vain: Four months later, the Oak Room's lunchtime men-only policy was rescinded without fanfare, around the same time that Betty Friedan got a divorce.

Mrs. Aristotle Onassis

*F*our days after the NOW protest, the snow still lay on the ground as Mrs. Aristotle Onassis, followed by her son and husband, exited Trader Vic's. The Onassises, newlyweds of four months, were the most famous couple in the world at the time. While most people portrayed at The Plaza were quite happy to have their picture taken there, this couple proved to be unwilling subjects, due to a new kind of photography—the paparazzi shot—which had come into being in the fifties. In this picture, Mrs. Onassis has donned her protective armor (oversize sunglasses, turned head, rueful half smile), but her husband appears not to have spotted the interloper yet. (Perhaps he is thinking of his own connection to The Plaza—he met his first wife, Tina Livanos, at a bridge game in one of the hotel's suites in 1943.)

The Easter Island tiki heads positioned under the far marquee, just above the snowball-toting John F. Kennedy, Jr., were installed when Trader Vic's opened in The Plaza's basement in 1965. Unpopular with Plaza regulars from the start, who felt that they weren't in keeping with the hotel's dignity—and put into place before the hotel became a designated landmark—the heads were removed without protest after Trader Vic's closed in 1993.

This page, clockwise from top left: Jane Fonda and Robert Redford in *Barefoot in the Park,* Paul Hogan in *Crocodile Dundee,* and Tom Hanks in *Joe Versus the Volcano.* Opposite, George Hamilton in *Love at First Bite,* Robert Redford and Barbra Streisand in *The Way We Were,* and Dudley Moore and Anne De Salvo in *Arthur.*

The Movies and The Plaza

As public fascination with the world of moviemaking and moviemakers grew over the century, filming at The Plaza kept pace. The hotel's popularity as a location is easily understood, for it served as shorthand for a certain kind of upscale urbanity; placing fictional characters in its environs made audiences immediately aware that the characters had style, sophistication, and money—or at least aspired to having those things.

Indeed, so many films were made on-site that The Plaza has inspired its own set of movie trivia. Some examples: Most appearances by an actor: Robert Redford (*Barefoot in the Park, The Way We Were, The Great Gatsby*). Most appearances by an actress: Whoopi Goldberg (*Soapdish, Eddie, The Associate*). Most appearances by a director: Sidney Lumet (*Network, Just Tell Me What You Want, Prince of the City*). Most appearances by a studio: Paramount (with eight films to date). Most common Plaza location shot: the Fifth Avenue entrance (with twenty-two appearances to date). Movies in which the hotel serves as the central setting: *Plaza Suite, Brewster's Millions, Big Business, Home Alone 2.* Movie that opens with scenes at the hotel: *Soapdish.* Movies that close at the hotel: *Plaza Suite, The Way We Were.*

Ironically enough, The Plaza doesn't appear at all in 1978's *I Wanna Hold Your Hand,* a dramatization of the Beatles' notorious first visit to the United States. The hotel refused the production company permission to shoot on-site (perhaps remembering all too well the tumult that the real event had caused), and the movie was shot instead with Boston's Copley Plaza standing in for The Plaza, an apt enough choice, as both buildings were designed by Henry Hardenbergh.

For a detailed filmography, see page 167.

The Green Tulip Debacle

One of The Plaza's few missteps over the years occurred in October 1971 when the Edwardian Room was closed and remade into the Green Tulip restaurant. And so, unbelievably, the stately room was redone in a color scheme of hot-pink and lime green, ersatz Tiffany lamps were installed, the dark wood paneling was painted over in a lighter shade, and potted plants and trees were added. Waitresses were hired for the first time, strolling folksingers roamed the floor, and after 10:00 P.M. the room was transformed into the Hot House at the Green Tulip, complete with disco dancing.

It was a disaster from the start. The potted trees died and were repeatedly replaced, the discotheque experiment drew few dancers, and angry mail began to arrive from aghast regular patrons. It all came to a head when *New York Times* architecture critic Ada Louise Huxtable published a scathing review of the room: "It adulterates the Plaza," she wrote, "to look and feel like any number of other older, big city hotels with residual grandeur, cheapened with tricksy restaurants full of familiar and rather loathsome design gimmicks and arch menus and publicity to match. This is meant to appeal, I assume, to a clientele that equates style with novelty and foolish elaboration, and wit with turgid coyness, and for whom the artifacts of the Edwardian era are less familiar than the surface of the moon."

The hotel got the message and the experiment was abandoned in May 1974. Below, the mock-funeral announcement sent out to mark its closing. At left, patrons sample a seventies staple, fondue, served by a waiter wearing a Donald Brooks–designed uniform.

The Plaza

announces with mock
sorrow and little regret,
the timely passing of
its restaurant,
THE GREEN TULIP
1971-1974
No flowers, please.
Donations can be made in
the form of patronage
to its successor,
THE PLAZA RESTAURANT
Opening June 18, 1974

John and Yoko in the Oyster Bar

$\mathcal{T}$he Oyster Bar at The Plaza, as it is officially known, opened on December 17, 1969, in the space that was originally a staff dining room and later the Hitchcock Pharmacy, the in-house drugstore. Designed in the style of an English seaside pub, with the liberal use of mahogany and etched glass, the Oyster Bar was the least formal of the hotel's dining rooms (that is, no jacket required), reflecting the casual era that had spawned it. Its relaxed ambience made it the preferred Plaza hangout for the latest breed of American celebrity, the rock star.

One of the most famed rockers, former Beatle John Lennon and his wife, the artist Yoko Ono, were among the room's regular patrons. In the fall of 1980, photographer Lilo Raymond was engaged to take pictures of the famed couple, who had emigrated to New York a few years earlier and were in the process of making a collaborative recording, later released as *Double Fantasy*. Raymond spent a day wandering the city with them, and just before repairing to the recording studio, she photographed them having lunch in a favorite haunt.

The inescapable poignance of this picture comes with hindsight, for John Lennon had only several months to live. He would be murdered in front of the Dakota apartment building on December 8, 1980.

Donald Trump Buys The Plaza

The Plaza's tradition of colorful, larger-than-life owners continued when real estate tycoon Donald Trump purchased the hotel in July 1988 for the sum of $390 million. Young, rich, and brash, Trump was one of the most visible millionaires in town, and reaction to his purchase echoed the reception given Conrad Hilton forty-five years earlier: general coolness from the old guard, who braced themselves for a lowering of standards. These fears proved groundless, however; like Hilton, Trump revitalized the hotel, and his tenure marked a rebirth for the property.

From the onset, Trump admitted to having paid too much for The Plaza. "This isn't just a building," he told the press. "It's the ultimate work of art—it's the Mona Lisa. I'm in love with it." In partnership with his wife, Ivana (who was named hotel president at a salary of "one dollar per year and all the dresses she can buy"), Trump undertook a meticulous, costly renovation of the lobby and banquet areas. In addition, six specialty suites—luxe echoes of Serge Obolensky's earlier celebrity versions—were created, as well as Gauguin, a restaurant-cum-discotheque that took over the space (and much of the decor) of the former Trader Vic's.

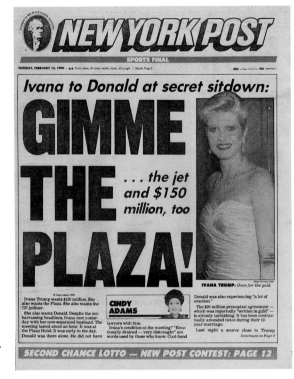

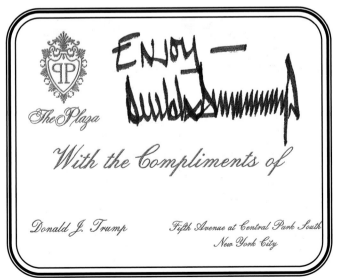

The heady atmosphere of the Trump era was short-lived, however, rocked by a stock market crash that forced the tycoon to pull in his reins, followed by a very public divorce from his wife (indeed, the breakup of the marriage was tabloid fodder for months, with The Plaza's name (above) lending a glamorous frisson to the proceedings). Trump eventually relinquished his interest in the property in 1995 to Prince Alwalid bin Talal bin Abdulaziz Saud, owner of the Fairmont Hotels, and CDL Hotels, a Singapore-based group, for $325 million.

Opposite, the Trumps during happier days at the Pulitzer Fountain. At left, a card that accompanied amenities sent by the owner.

Home Alone 2

*M*ovie sequels have long been a lucrative part of the motion picture business, and the 1990s sleeper hit *Home Alone* was a perfect candidate for a sequel. The original version recounted the misadventures of a youngster unintentionally left behind when his family went on vacation. After some complicated negotiations with The Plaza, the sequel repeated the formula with the boy at large, unchaperoned, in the world's most famous hotel.

The picture proved to be a marketing bonanza for the hotel (the actual telephone number for room reservations was announced twice in the dialogue), but the windfall came at no small price. Among other things, the Fifty-ninth Street lobby was shut down for several weeks, with check-in and other services relocated to the Fifth Avenue side for the duration of filming. Guests were still allowed the use of the Fifty-ninth Street elevators between takes, however, and many a surprised visitor alighted on the ground floor, only to find himself smack in the middle of a movie set.

Oddly enough, *Home Alone 2* was inadvertently responsible for a change in the lobby's overall appearance, which came

about during the shooting of a sequence that required actor Macaulay Culkin to slide across the floor into a waiting elevator (shown at left). To make the stunt possible, the film crew had been given permission to remove the wall-to-wall carpeting, in place at that time for about twenty-five years. When owner Donald Trump saw the exquisite mosaic-tile floor that lay underneath, he was so taken by it that wall-to-wall carpeting was banned thereafter, in favor of area rugs that allowed the mosaics to be seen again.

Above, Macaulay Culkin checks in; near left, the actor relaxes between takes.

Red Grooms at The Plaza

The work of American artist Red Grooms is not easily categorized—part burlesque and part opera, his multimedia assemblages are a mix of both Pop Art and Expressionist themes. *Ruckus Manhattan,* his most well-known piece, was completed in 1976. At right, his whimsical 1995 take on the hotel, naturally titled *The Plaza,* from Grooms's series of Fifth Avenue landmarks, *New York Stories.*

Photographs fail to convey Grooms's art very well; this work's three-dimensional effects and large scale (six feet by seven and a half) are somewhat diminished when reproduced on paper.

The Plaza Lighted for a Lingerie Show

*A*s the twentieth century came to an end, The Plaza endured, more renowned than ever due to a very high-profile movie career. Both the celebrated and the unsung continued to wed and be feted there, to dine and spend the night, to mark occasions both auspicious and inauspicious. Through it all, one of the most pervasive twentieth-century innovations—advertising—continued its ongoing association with the hotel.

To wit, the 1994 illumination of the building (right) to promote a fashion show sponsored by the lingerie manufacturer Victoria's Secret. The first runway show undertaken by the company, it quickly became a phenomenon when supermodels (the latest addition to the celebrity firmament) were engaged to model the lingerie. At once, the show was a hot ticket among power brokers, and indeed, the buzz reached such giddy heights that the show evolved into a full-blown media event, complete with televised coverage. Thus, the bathing of The Plaza in violet light to supply the press with a good visual lead-in to the story.

The last time the hotel had been so memorably illuminated was for the 1909 Hudson-Fulton celebration. One wonders what the next occasion will signify.

Time Line

The Plaza has been New York's most celebrated hotel for nearly a century. Designed by Henry J. Hardenbergh in the French Renaissance style, it opened on October 1, 1907. The hotel stands nineteen stories high, with over eight hundred guest rooms fitted with carved marble fireplaces, crystal chandeliers, ornamental plaster moldings, and mahogany doors. It currently houses four restaurants: the Oak Room, the Oak Bar, the Palm Court, and the Oyster Bar.

1863 • The Plaza's future site is a pond, the winter headquarters of the elite New York Skating Club.

1883– • Construction begins on first Plaza Hotel, on former site of the New York Skating Club; builders fail to raise
1889   funds to complete hotel and New York Life Insurance Company forecloses, hiring architects McKim, Mead and White to complete the hotel and redesign the interior.

1890 • First Plaza Hotel opens (October 1).

1892 • New Netherland Hotel and Savoy Hotel open opposite The Plaza on either side of Fifty-ninth Street.

1903 • Augustus Saint-Gaudens's statue of William Tecumseh Sherman unveiled in open plaza in front of hotel (May 30).

1905 • First Plaza Hotel demolished in order to build an even larger hotel (June).

1907 • New Plaza Hotel, constructed in twenty-seven months at a cost of $12.5 million, opens its doors (October 1).

• Taxi fleet makes its first appearance on New York streets, congregating at The Plaza and offering free rides to guests on opening day (October 1).

• First function held in Ballroom, a dinner hosted by the Pilgrims of America in honor of the Lord Bishop of London (October 15).

• Mrs. Patrick Campbell lights a cigarette in Palm Court, causing a scandal (November 15).

• Tenor Enrico Caruso checks in; the humming of the electric Magneta clock in his suite disturbs him, and he silences it with a knife, thereby stopping all the clocks in the hotel (December 8).

1908 • *Mrs. Van Vechten's Divorce Dance,* an amateur theatrical starring Mrs. George Jay Gould, staged in Ballroom (January 24).

• Russian Princess Vilma Lwoff-Parlaghy, noted portraitist and animal rights activist, checks in; later acquires lion cub that also takes up residence in hotel.

1909 • Chairs and tables removed from Fifty-eighth Street dining room (later the Rose Room) to convert it into a reading lounge.

- Plaza illuminated as part of citywide Hudson-Fulton Celebration; hotel is official host to foreign delegation from the Netherlands (September 25–October 11).

1910
- Lord Kitchener, British officer and statesman, stays at The Plaza during much-publicized visit to New York.
- Champagne Porch, an outdoor café along Fifth Avenue side of hotel, opens.
- Summer Garden, a seasonal restaurant, opens in the area later known as the Rose Room.

1912
- Mosaic tile floor in Rose Room replaced with hardwood floor, and space is used for tea dances and for private functions (until 1925).

1916
- Pulitzer Fountain dedicated (May).

1920
- Volstead Act closes Men's Bar (later becomes Oak Room).
- Men's Cafe (later Edwardian Room) is opened to women and renamed the Plaza Restaurant.
- Newlyweds Scott and Zelda Fitzgerald patronize the hotel's restaurants and Fitzgerald takes a much-publicized swim in the Pulitzer Fountain.

1921
- Construction of a three-hundred-room annex on the Fifth-eighth Street side of the hotel.
- Champagne Porch closes (June).
- New Fifth Avenue entrance constructed, and former dining room becomes Fifth Avenue lobby.
- Flags hung from Fifth Avenue side of hotel for the first time.
- New Ballroom opens (October 3).

1923
- Public square separating hotel from Fifth Avenue officially designated Grand Army Plaza by Board of Aldermen (February 10).
- Hotel builder Harry Black constructs duplex on eighteenth floor as his private apartment; later known as the Penthouse (October 1).

1925
- F. Scott Fitzgerald's novel *The Great Gatsby* published, with scenes set in hotel.
- Jessie Woolworth Donahue, heiress to the Woolworth fortune, has $683,000 worth of jewels stolen from her Plaza suite; gems are later recovered, with no questions asked; thief's identity is never known.
- Rose Room leased to Studebaker Corporation as showroom (December).

1927
- Plaza neighbor the Sherry-Netherland Hotel opens, replacing former New Netherland Hotel (September 29).

1928
- Plaza neighbor the Savoy-Plaza Hotel opens, replacing former Savoy Hotel.
- Plaza neighbor Bergdorf Goodman opens, replacing Cornelius Vanderbilt mansion.

1930
- Studebaker Corporation gives up showroom, and Rose Room reverts to space for private functions.

1930s
- Breaking up of large suites for permanent guests into rooms for visitors begins.

1933
- Prohibition is repealed (December).

1934
- Persian Room, an Art Moderne nightclub designed by Joseph Urban, opens in former Rose Room space (April 1).
- Oak Room, formerly the Men's Bar, opens as restaurant.

1938	• Pulitzer Fountain rebuilt due to deterioration.
1941– 1945	• Hotel enforces a three-day maximum stay during the war years (a citywide law due to room shortages), and it eventually places cots in offices to accommodate the overflow; countless bond drives launched in its public rooms.
1941	• Singer Hildegarde debuts in Persian Room; she will go on to make more appearances there than any other performer (September 23).
1943	• Conrad Hilton and Atlas Corporation acquire hotel for $7,400,000 (October).
1944	• Domed glass ceiling in Palm Court removed (November).
	• E. F. Hutton offices, adjacent to Oak Room, moved to mezzanine in Fifth Avenue lobby; construction of Oak Bar begins.
1945	• Oak Bar opens (January 13).
	• Murals painted by Everett Shinn installed in Oak Bar.
	• The Penthouse, Harry Black's former duplex, leased to *Gourmet* magazine as offices and test kitchen.
	• Center entrance of Fifty-ninth Street lobby sealed off and converted into flower shop.
1946	• Plaque honoring George M. Cohan installed in Oak Room by the Lambs, a theatrical club (April 24).
	• Greta Garbo photographed by Cecil Beaton in Suite 249–251 (April).
1947	• Hotel celebrates fortieth anniversary with party organized by Serge Obolensky (October 1).
	• Rendez-vous supper club opens in basement space formerly the Grill Room. (October 30).
	• Serge Obolensky introduces celebrity suites, specially designed apartments honoring couturier Christian Dior (223–225), photographer Cecil Beaton (249–251), novelist Somerset Maugham (649–651), and decorator Lady Mendl (317–325 and 501–503).
1950	• Industrial designer Henry Dreyfuss remodels Persian Room.
1951	• Singer Kay Thompson (future author of *Eloise*) and the Williams Brothers make first appearance in Persian Room (September 20).
1953	• Hotel sold to Park Fifty-ninth Street Corporation, headed by Boston industrialist A. M. Sonnabend, for $15 million (October 14).
	• Architect Frank Lloyd Wright moves into Suite 223–225, where he will live for the next six years as he supervises construction of Guggenheim Museum
	• Comedian Milton Berle celebrates his marriage to Ruth Cosgrove with reception at hotel (December 9).
1954	• State Suite opened to public as space for private functions.
	• Socialite Patricia Kennedy weds film star Peter Lawford and has reception in Ballroom (April 24).
1955	• *Eloise,* written by Kay Thompson and illustrated by Hilary Knight, is published.
	• Plaza Restaurant renamed and reopened as Edwardian Room.
1956	• Marilyn Monroe causes uproar at Terrace Room press conference when her shoulder strap breaks (February 9).

- Television sets installed in guest rooms for the first time.

- Tricycle Garage for children opens on 58th Street side of hotel (May).

- *Playhouse 90* special on Eloise airs on CBS (November 22).

1957
- Hotel celebrates fiftieth anniversary with dinner benefiting Recreation Service for Children of Bellevue (October 1).

- Hilary Knight's portrait of Eloise hung in lobby opposite Palm Court.

1958
- Trader Vic's opens in Savoy-Plaza Hotel (April 13).

- Alfred Hitchcock begins shooting *North by Northwest* in Oak Bar, marking hotel's movie debut (August).

- Miles Davis, Duke Ellington, and Billie Holiday perform at Persian Room private party hosted by Columbia Records; "Jazz at The Plaza," an original composition, is debuted by Davis (September 9).

- Hotel sold to lawyer and realty investor Lawrence A. Wein for $21 million; to be operated by Hotel Corporation of America (November 20).

1960
- Portrait of Eloise vanishes after college dance in Ballroom (November).

1961
- Rendez-vous supper club closes.

1962
- PLaza 9 cabaret opens in basement space formerly home of Rendez-vous.

1963
- New York Community Trust recognizes Plaza as landmark and affixes plaque to northeast corner of building.

- Fifty-eighth Street elevators converted from manned hydraulic cars to self-service electric.

- Singers Robert Goulet and Carol Lawrence are married in the State Suite (August 12).

- Palm Court After 8, a late-night dessert room, opens; staff includes the hotel's first waitresses (November 13).

1964
- Beatles arrive for a six-day visit (February 7).

- Beatles hold lively press conference in Baroque Room (February 10).

- New portrait of Eloise unveiled to coincide with New York World's Fair festivities (April 17).

1965
- Baroque Room enlarged, doubling its capacity.

- Demolition begins on Plaza neighbor, the Savoy-Plaza Hotel, which is replaced by General Motors Building.

- Trader Vic's transplanted from the Savoy-Plaza to The Plaza (August 18).

1966
- Author Truman Capote hosts legendary Black and White Ball in Ballroom (November 28).

1967
- Hassan II, King of Morocco, pays much-publicized six-day visit (February 11–17).

- Svetlana Alliluyeva, daughter of Joseph Stalin, holds Terrace Room press conference to explain her defection from Russia (April 26).

- Movie version of Neil Simon's play *Barefoot in the Park* released, with scenes shot on premises.

- *The Plaza: Its Life and Times,* by Eve Brown, published by Meredith Press.

1968
- Neil Simon's play *Plaza Suite* premieres at Broadway's Plymouth Theater (February 14).

- PLaza 9 . . . And All That Jazz opens, a reworking of the former cabaret into a jazz venue; opening act is Lionel Hampton (September 24).

- Julie Nixon, daughter of President-elect Richard Nixon, marries David Eisenhower and has reception in Ballroom (December 22).

1969
- Members of National Organization for Women, including its president, Betty Friedan, refused luncheon service in Oak Room, resulting in picket lines (February 12).
- Room 934 redesigned and opened as the Eloise Room (December 11).
- Hotel designated a New York City landmark by the Landmarks Preservation Commission (December).
- Oyster Bar opens (December 17).

1970
- PLaza 9 Music Hall opens in former PLaza 9 . . . And All That Jazz space; first show is *Dames at Sea* (September 22).
- Filming of *Plaza Suite* begins with location shooting in Fifty-ninth Street lobby (September 23).

1971
- Edwardian Room transformed into Green Tulip restaurant.
- Hotel acquired by Sonesta International.
- Ice Cream Corner opens in Fifty-eighth Street lobby (July).

1972
- Penthouse opened to public as space for nonresident guests for the first time.
- *The Plaza Cookbook,* by Eve Brown, published by Prentice-Hall.

1973
- Movie *The Way We Were* released, with scenes shot at Fifth Avenue entrance.
- Eloise Room closed.
- *Jazz at The Plaza,* a recording of 1958 Persian Room concert featuring Miles Davis, Duke Ellington, and Billie Holiday, released by Columbia Records.
- Twenty-four hour room service introduced (December 14).
- Persian Room redecorated.

1974
- Ice Cream Corner closes (March 31).
- Green Tulip restaurant closes (May 18).
- Plaza Restaurant opens in Green Tulip space (June 18); name later reverts to Edwardian Room.
- Grand Army Plaza designated New York City landmark.
- Film version of *The Great Gatsby* released, with scenes shot on premises.
- Western International Hotels acquires The Plaza for $25 million (November).

1975
- Persian Room closes, after a forty-one-year run.

1976
- Fifty-ninth Street elevators converted from manned hydraulic cars to self-service electric.

1977
- Cinema 3 movie theater opens in basement space formerly PLaza 9 Music Hall (January 24).

1978
- Plaza added to National Register of Historic Places by U.S. Department of the Interior (November 28).

1980
- Plaza added to New York State Register of Historic Places (June 23).

1981
- Western International Hotels renamed Westin.

- Movie *Arthur* released, with scene shot in Oak Room.

1982
- Hotel celebrates seventy-fifth anniversary with dinner benefiting New York Landmarks Conservancy (September 30).

1985
- The Plaza Accord—an international economic agreement—signed in Baroque Room by finance ministers of the United States, Japan, West Germany, Great Britain, and France (September 22).

- Nonsmoking rooms introduced.

1986
- The Plaza named National Historic Landmark (June 24).

- Movie *Crocodile Dundee* released, with scenes shot on premises.

1987
- Entire Westin chain (including The Plaza) sold to partnership of Robert M. Bass and the Aoki Corporation (October).

1988
- Tycoon Donald Trump acquires hotel for $390 million (July).

- Movie *Big Business* released, with scenes shot on premises.

1989
- Specialty suites designed under supervision of Ivana Trump: the Astor Suite (317–323), the Bridal Suite (1011–1013), the Vanderbilt (533–543), the Frank Lloyd Wright (221–223), the Louis XVI (1019–1023), and the Presidential (1801).

- *The Hotel: A Week in the Life of The Plaza,* by Sonny Kleinfield, published by Simon and Schuster.

1991
- Movie *Home Alone 2* begins filming in the Fifty-ninth Street lobby (December).

1992
- Movie *Scent of a Woman* released, with scene shot in Oak Room.

- Filmmaker Woody Allen declares his love for the daughter of his former companion at crowded Terrace Room press conference (August).

1993
- Actor Eddie Murphy weds Nicole Mitchell in Ballroom (March 18).

- Plaza owner Donald Trump weds actress Marla Maples in Ballroom (December 20).

- Trader Vic's closes.

1994
- Gauguin, a nightclub featuring tropical French cuisine, opens in basement space formerly occupied by Trader Vic's (June).

1995
- Plaza used as setting on an episode of *Seinfeld,* the nation's top-rated comedy (April 6).

- Hotel sold to Prince Alwalid bin Talal bin Abdulaziz Saud, owner of Fairmont Hotels, and CDL Hotels International for $325 million (July 28).

1996
- *A Plaza Wedding,* by Lawrence Harvey, published by Villard Books.

1997
- First female doorperson, Sheila Connors, begins work at the Fifth Avenue door (November).

- Cinema 3 closes.

1998
- Edwardian Room closes; space reverts to room for private functions.

2000
- Plaza Spa opens in lower-level space formerly occupied by Trader Vic's and Cinema 3.

Filmography

*A*lthough The Plaza appeared fleetingly in earlier films, the hotel made its true movie debut in Alfred Hitchcock's 1959 classic *North by Northwest*—the first time a crew, director, and cast assembled on this site to make a picture. Before then, movies had been shot almost entirely on Hollywood soundstages, rarely on location (The Plaza portrayed in films like *The Band Wagon* was solely the set designer's version of the place). Once cameras were freed from soundstages in the 1960s, the hotel appeared in so many pictures that it eventually became New York City's most popular movie location. As the following list attests, The Plaza has been muse to a far-reaching variety of filmmakers and films:

North by Northwest. 1959 (MGM). *Directed by Alfred Hitchcock. With Cary Grant and Eva Marie Saint.* (Scenes shot in Fifty-ninth Street lobby, Oak Bar, and guest corridor; hotel room re-created on soundstage.)

Man on a String. 1960 (Columbia). *Directed by André De Toth. With Ernest Borgnine and Colleen Dewhurst.*

Barefoot in the Park. 1967 (Paramount). *Directed by Gene Saks. With Robert Redford and Jane Fonda.* (Scenes shot in Fifty-ninth Street lobby and fourth-floor corridor.)

Plaza Suite. 1971 (Paramount). *Directed by Arthur Hiller. With Walter Matthau, Maureen Stapleton, Lee Grant, and Barbara Harris.* (Scenes shot at Fifth Avenue entrance, Fifty-ninth Street lobby, Baroque Room, and seventh-floor corridor; Plaza suite re-created on soundstage.)

The Way We Were. 1973 (Columbia). *Directed by Sydney Pollack. With Barbra Streisand and Robert Redford.* (Scenes shot at Fifth Avenue entrance.)

40 Carats. 1973 (Columbia). *Directed by Milton Katselas.* *With Liv Ullmann, Edward Albert, and Gene Kelly.* (Scenes shot at Fifth Avenue entrance, Fifty-ninth Street lobby, and seventh-floor corridor; Plaza suite re-created on soundstage.)

The Great Gatsby. 1974 (Paramount). *Directed by Jack Clayton. With Robert Redford and Mia Farrow.* (Scene shot at Fifth Avenue entrance; hotel interiors re-created at Pinewood Studios, London.)

Network. 1976 (MGM/United Artists). *Directed by Sidney Lumet. With Peter Finch, William Holden, and Faye Dunaway.* (Scenes shot in Ballroom and Ballroom foyer.)

The Front. 1976 (Columbia). *Directed by Martin Ritt. With Woody Allen and Zero Mostel.* (Scene shot in Plaza suite.)

King of the Gypsies. 1978 (Paramount). *Directed by Frank Pierson. With Eric Roberts, Judd Hirsch, and Susan Sarandon.* (Scene shot at Fifth Avenue entrance.)

The Rose. 1979 (Twentieth Century–Fox). *Directed by Mark Rydell. With Bette Midler and Alan Bates.* (Scene shot at Fifth Avenue entrance; Plaza room re-created on soundstage.)

Love at First Bite. 1979 (American International Pictures). *Directed by Stan Dragoti. With George Hamilton and Susan St. James.* (Scenes shot at Fifth Avenue entrance; Plaza suite re-created on soundstage.)

Just Tell Me What You Want. 1980 (Warner Bros.). *Directed by Sidney Lumet. With Ali MacGraw and Alan King.* (Scene shot in Palm Court.)

Arthur. 1981 (Warner Bros./Orion). *Directed by Steve Gordon. With Dudley Moore and Liza Minnelli.* (Scenes shot at Fifth Avenue entrance and Oak Room.)

Prince of the City. 1981 (Warner Bros./Orion). *Directed by Sidney Lumet. With Treat Williams and Jerry Orbach.* (Scene shot in Plaza suite.)

They All Laughed. 1981 (Moon Pictures). *Directed by Peter Bogdanovich. With Audrey Hepburn, Ben Gazzara, and John Ritter.* (Scenes shot in Palm Court and Fifth Avenue and Fifty-ninth Street lobbies.)

Paternity. 1981 (Paramount). *Directed by David Steinberg. With Burt Reynolds and Beverly D'Angelo.* (Scenes shot at Fifth Avenue entrance and Oak Bar.)

Author! Author! 1982 (Twentieth Century–Fox). *Directed by Arthur Hiller. With Al Pacino and Dyan Cannon.* (Scene shot in Palm Court.)

The Cotton Club. 1984 (Zoetrope Studios). *Directed by Francis Coppola. With Richard Gere and Gregory Hines.* (Scene shot in Plaza suite.)

Unfaithfully Yours. 1984. (Twentieth Century–Fox). *Directed by Howard Zieff. With Dudley Moore and Natassja Kinski.* (Scene shot at Fifth Avenue entrance; Plaza suite re-created on soundstage.)

Brewster's Millions. 1985 (Universal). *Directed by Walter Hill. With Richard Pryor and John Candy.* (Scenes shot at Fifth Avenue entrance and Fifty-ninth Street lobby; Plaza suite re-created on soundstage.)

Crocodile Dundee. 1986 (Paramount). *Directed by Peter Faiman. With Paul Hogan and Linda Kozlowski.* (Scenes shot at Fifth Avenue entrance and Fifty-ninth Street lobby; Plaza suite re-created on soundstage.)

Big Business. 1988 (Touchstone). *Directed by Jim Abrahams. With Bette Midler and Lily Tomlin.* (Scenes shot at Fifth Avenue entrance and Fifty-ninth Street facade; hotel interiors re-created on soundstage.)

The January Man. 1989 (MGM). *Directed by Pat O'Connor. With Kevin Kline, Mary Elizabeth Mastrantonio, and Susan Sarandon.* (Scene shot at Fifth Avenue entrance.)

Soapdish. 1991 (Paramount). *Directed by Michael Hoffman. With Sally Field, Kevin Kline, and Whoopi Goldberg.* (Opening scene shot at Fifth Avenue entrance.)

Regarding Henry. 1991 (Paramount). *Directed by Mike Nichols. With Harrison Ford and Annette Bening.* (Scenes shot in Oak Room and Edwardian Room.)

Scent of a Woman. 1992 (MCA/Universal). *Directed by Martin Brest. With Al Pacino and Chris O'Donnell.* (Scene shot in Oak Room.)

Home Alone 2. 1992 (Twentieth Century–Fox). *Directed by Chris Columbus. With Macaulay Culkin and Joe Pesci.* (Scenes shot in Fifth Avenue and Fifty-ninth Street lobbies, fourth-floor corridor, and Suite 411.)

Sleepless in Seattle. 1993 (Tristar). *Directed by Nora Ephron. With Tom Hanks and Meg Ryan.* (Scene shot at

Fifth Avenue entrance; Plaza room re-created on soundstage.)

The Pickle. 1993 (Columbia). *Directed by Paul Mazursky. With Danny Aiello and Dyan Cannon.* (Scenes shot at Fifth Avenue entrance, Fifth Avenue and Fifty-ninth Street lobbies, and Oak Bar; Plaza suite re-created on soundstage.)

It Could Happen to You. 1994 (Tristar). *Directed by Andrew Bergman. With Nicolas Cage and Bridget Fonda.* (Scenes shot at Fifth Avenue entrance, Fifty-ninth Street lobby and entrance, eighth-floor corridor, and Suite 811.)

Eddie. 1996 (Hollywood/Island/Polygram). *Directed by Steve Rash. With Whoopi Goldberg and Frank Langella.* (Scene shot at Fifth Avenue entrance.)

The Associate. 1996 (Buena Vista/Hollywood/Polygram). *Directed by Donald Petrie. With Whoopi Goldberg and Dianne Wiest.* (Scenes shot at Fifth Avenue entrance, Fifth Avenue and Fifty-ninth Street lobbies, Palm Court, and Vanderbilt Suite.)

For Richer or Poorer. 1997 (MCA/Universal). *Directed by Brian Spicer. With Tim Allen and Kirstie Alley.* (Scenes shot at Fifth Avenue entrance and Grand Ballroom.)

Cameo Appearances

Gentleman's Agreement (1947), scene shot in Grand Army Plaza. *The Band Wagon* (1953), mentioned in dialogue; Plaza suite re-created on soundstage. *Woman's World* (1954), Plaza suite re-created on soundstage. *Midnight Cowboy* (1969), scene shot in Grand Army Plaza; mentioned in dialogue. *John and Mary* (1969), mentioned in dialogue. *I Wanna Hold Your Hand* (1978), mentioned in dialogue. *Two of a Kind* (1983), Palm Court re-created on soundstage. *Joe Versus the Volcano* (1990), brief view at Fifty-ninth Street entrance; mentioned in dialogue. *The Money Train* (1996), scene shot in Grand Army Plaza. *Mission Impossible* (1996), mentioned in dialogue. *Mighty Aphrodite* (1995), mentioned in dialogue. *Everyone Says I Love You* (1996), Plaza suite used as stand-in for hotel suite in Venice.

Bibliography

For further reading about The Plaza, inquire at your library about the following titles.

Books

Primary Sources

Brown, Eve. *The Plaza: Its Life and Times.* New York: Meredith Press, 1967. The only general history of the hotel, written by its former head of publicity.

————. *The Plaza Cookbook.* New York: Prentice-Hall, 1972. More than three hundred recipes from the hotel's kitchens, along with culinary anecdotes.

Harris, Bill. *The Plaza.* Secaucus: Poplar Books, 1981. A large-format picture book, with many contemporary color photos.

Harvey, Lawrence D. *A Plaza Wedding.* New York: Villard Books, 1996. The story of weddings at the hotel, written by its executive director of catering.

Kleinfield, Sonny. *The Hotel: A Week in the Life of The Plaza.* New York: Simon and Schuster, 1989. A journalistic look at the hotel over a seven-day period.

Secondary Sources

Arnold, Eve. *Marilyn Monroe.* New York: Alfred A. Knopf, 1987, pp. 63–67. An illustrated account of the actress's notorious press conference in the Terrace Room.

Bogart, Michele H. *Public Sculpture and the Civil Ideal in New York City, 1890–1930.* Chicago: University of Chicago Press, 1989, pp. 185–193; 205–217. An account of the construction of the Pulitzer Fountain.

Brown, Henry Collins. *Fifth Avenue Old and New, 1824–1924.* New York: Fifth Avenue Association, 1924, p. 87. Description of the Plaza site in 1863, when it was home to the New York Skating Club.

Dabney, Thomas Ewing. *The Man Who Bought the Waldorf.* New York: Duell, Sloan and Pearce, 1950, pp. 154–174. A life of Conrad Hilton, with an account of his purchase of The Plaza in 1943.

DeShazo, Edith. *Everett Shinn.* New York: Clarkson Potter, 1974, pp. 100, 104–111. Illustrations of the three murals painted by the artist for the Oak Bar.

Guerrero, Pedro E. *Picturing Wright.* San Francisco: Pomegranate, 1994, pp. 137–143, 156–157. Reminiscences about Frank Lloyd Wright's years as a Plaza permanent guest, along with pictures of his apartment in the hotel.

Hennessee, Judith. *Betty Friedan: Her Life.* New York: Random House, 1999, pp. 121–122. An account of the National Organization for Women's 1969 sit-in in the Oak Room.

Hilton, Conrad. *Be My Guest.* New York: Prentice Hall, 1957. Autobiography of the hotelier, with a short account of his 1943 purchase of The Plaza.

Obolensky, Serge. *One Man in His Time.* New York: McDowell, Obolensky, 1958. Memoirs of The Plaza's postwar public-relations and promotion director.

Plimpton, George. *Truman Capote.* New York: Doubleday, 1997, pp. 248–278. An oral history of the writer's life, with reminiscences about his Black and White Ball.

Reynolds, Donald Martin. *The Architecture of New York City.* New York: John Wylie and Sons, 1994, pp. 184–188. Concise architectural overview of the hotel.

Souhami, Diana. *Greta & Cecil.* San Francisco: HarperSanFrancisco, 1994, pp. 147–151, 162–178. The story behind the 1946 Cecil Beaton photographs made of Greta Garbo in Room 249.

Stern, Robert A. M. *New York 1900.* New York: Rizzoli, 1983, pp. 258–262. Architectural analysis of the building, part of a general history of turn-of-the-century hotels.

Tauranac, John, and Christopher Little. *Elegant New York.* New York: Abbeville Press, 1985, pp. 150–155. A history of The Plaza and its builders.

Periodicals

Brenner, Marie. "Kay and Eloise." *Vanity Fair,* December 1996, pp. 297–313. A biography of Kay Thompson, author of *Eloise.*

Collins, Amy Fine. "A Night to Remember." *Vanity Fair,* July 1996, pp. 120–139. An account of Truman Capote's 1966 Black and White Ball.

Crowninshield, Frank. "Up on Central Park." *Vogue,* October 1, 1947, pp. 196, 242–243. An appreciation written on the occasion of The Plaza's fortieth anniversary.

Frazier, George. "Elegance Entrenched." *Esquire,* January 1956, pp. 79–80. An appreciation and short history of the hotel.

Goldberger, Paul. "At 75, Plaza Hotel Seeks to Remain Old Forever." *New York Times,* September 27, 1982. *New York Times* architecture critic on The Plaza's seventy-fifth birthday.

————. "A Spot of Paint Won't Hurt This Lily." *New York Times,* January 22, 1989. Speculation on the hotel's future after its sale to Donald Trump.

Gray, Christopher. "Grand Hotel." *Avenue,* September 1988, pp. 76–88. An analysis of the hotel over the years.

Meyers, William H. "The Great Plaza Plot: The Jockeying for One of the World's Great Hotels." *New York Times Magazine,* September 25, 1988. The story of Donald Trump's acquisition of the hotel.

Molnar, Ferenc. "The Plaza." *Park East,* June 1950, pp. 10–11. A memoir by the noted Hungarian writer and Plaza permanent guest.

Muschamp, Herbert. "Taliesin the Third." *House & Garden,* October 1983, pp. 40, 44. A description with color photographs of the suite occupied by Frank Lloyd Wright from 1953–1959.

"Another Fine Hotel Now On the City's List." *New York Times,* September 29, 1907. An introduction to the new hotel, published just prior to its opening.

————. "The Plaza: A Genteel Hotel is a New York Tradition." *Life,* November 18, 1946, pp. 86–93. Photo essay on newly renovated hotel under Conrad Hilton's supervision.

Warren, Virginia Lee. "Fitzgerald's Plaza Sheds Its Cobwebs." *New York Times,* December 25, 1966. A profile of the hotel in the mid-1960s.

Works of Fiction with Plaza Settings

DeLillo, Don. *Underworld.* New York: Scribner, 1997. Gives imaginary account of J. Edgar Hoover attending Truman Capote's party.

Fitzgerald, F. Scott. *The Great Gatsby.* New York: Scribner, 1925. Fitzgerald's masterpiece incorporates the Palm Court and a Plaza suite as settings.

Simon, Neil. *Plaza Suite.* New York: Random House, 1969. The long-running play, observing three sets of guests who inhabit the same hotel suite.

Thompson, Kay. *Kay Thompson's Eloise: The Absolutely Essential Edition.* New York: Simon & Schuster, 1955. The children's classic, with an added scrapbook detailing the lives of the author and the book's illustrator, Hilary Knight.

Illustration Credits

All illustrated material in this book is drawn from The Plaza Archives, with the following exceptions:

Acknowledgments

The generous cooperation of the following individuals helped make this book possible: Lynda Castillo, Tom Civitano, Joe Cleemann, Antonio Diaz, Pedro Guerrero, Don Hunstein, Eliot Selznick Hubbard, Ken Royer, Sid Kaplan, Christina Krupka, Jay Mulvaney, Tom Norberg, Lilo Raymond, James Sinclair, Alfred G. Vanderbilt, Jr., and Bert Yaeger.

In addition, special thanks to my editor, Charles Spicer, for his enthusiasm and support; Rose Ganguzza for making the introductions at St. Martin's Press; Anna Mogyorosy, for incomparable photo research; and Gary Schweikert, The Plaza's general manager, for allowing me access to the hotel's archives. Indeed, Mr. Schweikert's commitment to this project is ultimately what brought it to life.

Index

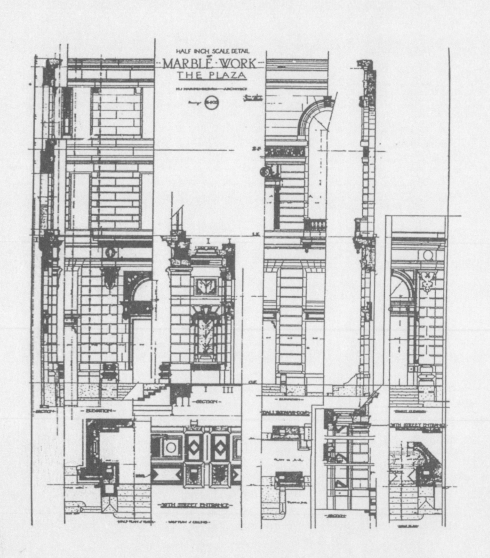